PHONIC REMEDIAL READING LESSONS

SAMUEL A. KIRK, PhD
WINIFRED D. KIRK, MA
ESTHER H. MINSKOFF, PhD

Academic Therapy Publications
Novato, California

Academic Therapy Publications
20 Commercial Boulevard
Novato, California 94949-6191

International Standard Book Number: 0-87879-508-1

6 5 4 3 2 1 0 9
5 4 3 2 1 0 9 8 7

Contents

Part II
Two or More Letters, One Sound

Part III
Consonant Blends and Other Shortcuts

Part IV
New Configurations

Part V
Exceptions to Configurations Previously Taught

Part VI
Word Building and Syllabication

TEACHING GUIDE TO THE PHONIC REMEDIAL READING LESSONS

The *Phonic Remedial Reading Lessons* provide a systematic, programmed method of teaching reading to children who have failed to learn to read by the experience, language, basal reader, or look-and-say methods commonly used in schools.

These reading lessons are based on the *Remedial Reading Drills* by Thorleif G. Hegge, Samuel A. Kirk, and Winifred D. Kirk, which were devised for teaching reading to reading disabled students who were mildly mentally retarded. Since their publication in 1936, the *Remedial Reading Drills* have been used successfully with children of low, average, and even superior intelligence. Since the basic strategies used in the *Remedial Reading Drills* have proven effective in more than fifty years of use, these strategies have been retained in the *Phonic Remedial Reading Lessons.* The modifications made in this new program are based on suggestions for improvement made over many years by teachers and clinicians who have used the Hegge, Kirk, and Kirk *Remedial Reading Drills.*

The *Phonic Remedial Reading Lessons* are not recommended as a general technique for teaching beginning reading. Most children learn to read with little tutelage and much exposure to appropriate reading material. They develop their own decoding skills and do not require intensive instruction in learning to read. There is a small percentage of children, however, who struggle for years without grasping the knack of translating printed symbols into meaningful concepts. Such children have more difficulty in learning to read than is expected from their accomplishments in other areas. They are generally labeled reading disabled or dyslexic. These children usually require a systematic, step-by-step procedure utilizing an intensive phonics approach based on valid strategies of learning.

Children for Whom the Lessons are Most Suitable

Children for whom the *Phonic Remedial Reading Lessons* are most suitable have the following characteristics:

1. They are seven and one-half or more years of age, and have been in school for at least one year.
2. They have adequate overall mental ability to learn to read. This does not mean that their intelligence is necessarily average, since most slow learning and mildly mentally retarded children of nine or ten years of age may have sufficient mental ability to learn to read.
3. They have developed sufficient oral language to be understood and sufficient receptive language to understand second- or third-grade material when it is read to them.
4. They have an educationally significant reading problem as evidenced by a discrepancy between reading grade and the grade expectancy based on their mental development, language performance, and arithmetic ability.
5. They have not yet learned an efficient method of decoding new words. The reading level of the child should be third grade or below, since any child who can read above this level has already learned a method of decoding new words. Reading disabled children who have attained fourth grade or more in reading and have learned decoding skills need a different remedial approach.
6. They do not have any uncorrected auditory or visual deficiencies that could interfere with adequate perception.
7. They must be receptive to motivation for learning, especially in an individual or small group situation. At the outset of remediation or in the classroom, some reading disabled children have appeared uncooperative and uninterested. In many cases, after they achieved some degree of success, they cooperated fully. Usually a child who has failed to learn to read in the regular classroom is very conscious of his disability and is apt to reject attempts to teach him. Any method which shows him early success, however, is likely to be accepted.

Guiding Principles of the *Phonic Remedial Reading Lessons*

The *Phonic Remedial Reading Lessons* are a unique remedial program that differs from other phonic programs in its consistent and expanding development of phonic usage and its application of certain underlying principles of learning. The strategies employed include: (a) strategies built into the program, and (b) strategies in the method or presentation.

Built-in Strategies

1. *One response to one symbol.* One basic instructional strategy which is built into the *Phonic Remedial Reading Lessons* is that only one response is required for each visual symbol. The letter **a**, for example, is taught only as the short **a** as in **man.** When the letter **a** is found in combination with another vowel, as **oa** in **boat** or **ay** in **may**, that configuration is taught as a single unit. Each configuration is taught with

a specific sound association. This avoids the child's having to go through the process of deciding which of two sounds to use. These configurations of two letters taught as one sound unit are separated in the lessons from the other letters of a word at first to indicate that they represent a single sound.

2. *Minimal change.* Built into the lessons is the principle of minimal change to promote consistent success. As will be seen in Lesson 1, the first section of each lesson presents a series of words **(sat, mat,** etc.) in which only the initial consonant changes. The second section retains the initial sound and changes only the last consonant. The third section changes both the initial and final consonants. Thus, within each lesson a step-by-step procedure is followed. The child thereby attends to only one increment at a time, thus promoting errorless responses, providing for a feeling of success, and increasing motivation.

3. *Progress from easy to hard.* The lessons are sequentially organized, going from easy to difficult. The easiest sounds are taught initially, and after these are mastered the more difficult sounds are introduced.

4. *Frequent repetition.* Extensive repetition in varied situations is used. Both research and practical experience have indicated that it is necessary for the reading disabled child to have many repetitions of the same concept in varied forms to master the target sounds and words. The sound-symbol association must become automatic.

5. *Review.* Frequent reviews are also programmed into the lessons so that overlearning may take place. The first two lessons present only the sound of short **a** together with most of the consonants. The third lesson presents only the sound of short **o**. The fourth lesson presents both **a** and **o**.

6. *Verbal mediation.* Based on the principle that the child's own verbal expression aids learning, the lessons require oral responses from the child for each phoneme and each word.

7. *Multisensory learning.* In learning each new phoneme, the child is instructed to visualize, write, say, and hear the sounds simultaneously, thus providing for the involvement of the visual, kinesthetic, vocal, and auditory channels. This is what we refer to as the grapho-vocal method which will be described later.

Strategies in Methods of Presentation

1. *Knowledge of results.* To obtain immediate knowledge of results the oral response of the child helps him to hear the sound or the word as he says it. The teacher, when necessary, confirms the response by repeating what the child has said if it is correct. If it is not correct, the teacher should provide the correct model for the child and ask him to repeat it.

2. *Social reinforcement* (praise) should be used frequently for correct responses given by the child in the early stages of learning. When some mastery has been achieved,

intermittent reinforcement can be given. It is especially important for the child to realize that he is indeed learning to read.

3. *Selective attention.* These phonic lessons are based on the premise that it is necessary to train a child's selective attention to the relevant cues for reading different types of words. Therefore, the spacing between letters indicates to the child that he is to attend to each symbol and to sound the different letters in order to read the word. Individual instruction aids the process of attention.

4. *No rules* are taught in the *Phonic Remedial Reading Lessons.* The system is so organized that an automatic verbal response is made to the visual symbols and corrected when necessary. The responses become automatic and not dependent on verbalized rules.

5. *Individualized instruction.* The lessons are designed for individual instruction, one teacher to one child. In this situation, attention is controlled and the child progresses at his own rate. Under limited conditions a small group of two or three children can work together if they have sufficient individual instruction and are able to progress together in the same lesson.

6. *Nonphonic words are taught as wholes.* Sight words which are not to be sounded are gradually introduced in accompanying sentences and stories. Procedures for teaching these are given in the lessons and in a later section.

7. *The printed material beginning with Lesson 1 is never presented until the child has reached a level of readiness.* This involves (a) auditory discrimination of sounds, (b) auditory sound-blending ability, and (c) sound-symbol association for the vowel **a** and most of the common consonants. Each of these prerequisites can be assessed formally or informally, or both. If a child is found deficient in any of these prerequisite skills, the skill must be systematically taught.

How to Use the *Phonic Remedial Reading Lessons*

In addition to the two types of strategies described in the preceding section, the teacher should bear in mind the following steps in presenting the lessons.

Developing the Readiness Level

Visual discrimination in recognizing differences among the letters of the English language is usually not a major problem in learning to read. Some children with attention difficulties or marked visual perceptual problems may need specific attention to this problem. The grapho-vocal method as described later is applicable here.

It should be remembered that auditory discrimination and sound blending do not require visual cues. They are purely auditory/vocal functions. Once a child can differentiate the sounds spoken orally and can blend sounds to form words, then visual symbols may be associated with the sounds he or she hears or speaks.

Auditory Discrimination. A child must be able to differentiate between similar sounds in isolation (e.g., /**t**/ vs. /**d**/) and also in words (e.g., **pin** vs. **pen**). Auditory discrimination can be formally assessed with the Wepman Auditory Discrimination Test (Palm Springs, CA: Language Research Associates, 1973), or informally by the teacher.

When informally assessing auditory discrimination, the teacher should say: "I'm going to say two words that are not the same. Pin. Cat. They are not the same. Now I'm going to say some words and you tell me if they are the same or not the same." Use the 20 word pairs listed below. To avoid any lip reading cues, do not allow the child to look at your lips as you say the words on the test. You should cover your mouth but maintain eye contact with the child.

1. bug - top
2. hop - tip
3. pig - pot
4. luck - luck
5. cat - cap
6. pig - pin
7. map - map
8. red - red
9. cat - cab
10. nut - nut
11. wig - dig
12. tin - tin
13. mat - met
14. well - will
15. beg - big
16. him - him
17. dig - big
18. nail - mail
19. get - get
20. kid - kit

If a child seems to be markedly deficient in this ability and fails more than four or five of these, then provide training in auditory discrimination before using the *Phonic Remedial Reading Lessons.* Unless the child is markedly deficient, he will probably improve in this ability once he has begun the lessons. As an instructional aid in the beginning, it is sometimes helpful to have the child look at your lips to get visual cues and to have him repeat each word after you to get kinesthetic cues. As the child masters the discrimination tasks, eliminate these instructional aids.

Auditory Sound Blending. At the readiness stage in the use of the *Phonic Remedial Reading Lessons,* it is necessary for the child to be able to blend sounds into words, **c a t** = **cat.** Until a child can acquire this facility of gaining auditory closure from a sequence of sounds, he cannot utilize phonic clues to decode a word. Sound blending can be assessed informally by having students give the complete word for the sounds spoken with one-second intervals between the separated sounds.

When informally assessing sound blending, say to the child: "I'm going to say some words very slowly, and I want you to tell me what word I am saying. Listen—/**sh**/**oe**/. What did I say?" Each letter sound should be made as it is heard in the word, and the sounds should be given at one-second intervals. Use this same procedure for each word on the list on the following page.

1. /sh/oe/
2. /m/e/
3. /g/o/
4. /c/a/t/
5. /f/a/n/
6. /p/o/t/
7. /s/i/t
8. /p/e/t/
9. /s/t/o/p/
10. /s/a/n/d/
11. /f/l/a/t/
12. /j/u/m/p/

If a child seems to be markedly deficient in sound blending and fails to synthesize words with three or four sounds, then auditory training in sound blending should be provided. In such training, the teacher must attend to two factors. One factor is the duration of time between sounds; the other is the number of sounds in a sequence. When a word is sounded with practically no duration between the sounds, it is much easier for a child to blend the sounds than if a word is presented with one-second intervals between the sounds. Therefore, in the early stages of training, provide a very small interval between sounds and gradually make it longer until a one-second interval is reached. Sounds which can be prolonged (e.g., **s, f, m**) should be used at first.

The other factor to be programmed into the training is the number of sounds in a word. The more sounds used, the harder it is for the child to remember and synthesize them. First present words with two sounds (**/sh/oe/**), and then words with three sounds (**/c/a/t**), and finally words with four sounds (**/s/a/n/d/**).

To train a child in sound blending, use the following procedure.

Teacher: "Say shoe."

Child: "Shoe."

Teacher: "Now, what am I saying? **/sh-sh-sh/oo-oo-oo/**." (Say it with prolonged sounds, but no break between the sounds.) If the child responds correctly, say: "Good. Now what am I saying?" (Give a little break between the sounds.) "**/Sh/oe/**." Then say (with the child), "Shoe. Now what am I saying?" (Give a quarter-second break between the sounds.) "**/Sh/oe/**."

Child: "Shoe."

Teacher: "Shoe. Good. What am I saying now?" (with a half-second break between the sounds) "**/Sh/oe/**."

Child: "Shoe."

Teacher: "Now what am I saying?" (give a one-second break between the sounds) "**/Sh/oe/**."

At each step, if the child does not respond with "shoe," repeat the previous step and then again stretch out the sounds, confirming or prompting at each step. Proceed by increasing the duration until the child can say "shoe" in response to the sounds with approximately one second between them.

Repeat this experience with the word "me."

The main task for the teacher is to give a word with two sounds, increasing the duration of time between them until the child gets the idea of putting the sounds together. Then the child is presented with three-sound words such as **/f/a/t/**, and then with four-sounds words such as **/s/a/n/d/**. It is important to recognize that the number of sounds in a word may not correspond to the number of letters in a word. For example, the word "shoe" has four letters, but only two sounds. The teacher must be careful to present the sounds correctly and use the correct timing.

Sound blending is the most often neglected aspect of a phonic approach to remedial reading. It is an essential prerequisite to beginning the *Phonic Remedial Reading Lessons.*

Sound-Symbol Association. Before beginning Lesson 1, it is necessary to teach or at least expose the child to the sounds of the short vowel **a**, and the 11 consonants included in Lesson 1A. To teach the child the sound-symbol association and the use of the sounds in decoding words, proceed as follows:

1. Write the letter **a** and say to the child, "This letter sounds **'a'** like a baby crying . . . **a-a-a-a.** Say **'a.'** Now write it and say **'a.'** " (short vowel)

2. After the child has written the **a** and sounded the letter correctly, proceed to teach the sounds of the letters **s** (in snake), **t** (a clock ticking), **p** (pop!), and **m** (tastes good—mmm). Then have the child write each letter and sound it at the same time. This is the grapho-vocal method, writing while saying the sound simultaneously. Always confirm a correct response with "Yes, **'t,'** " or "Yes, **'m'**."

3. To show the child that sounds of letters form words, write **s,** asking the child to sound it, then **a,** and then **t,** asking the child to sound each one. Ask the child to sound the letters again, in sequence, "**s a t, sat.**" Then say, "This is the way we can learn to read. Now let's see how many words you can read by sounding them."

   Write the following words, one at a time, asking the child to sound each letter separately and to blend the sounds into a word. When he sounds and reads three words say, "See, when we know the sounds of a few letters we can read many words."

s a t	sat
p a t	pat
m a t	mat
t a p	tap
s a p	sap
m a p	map
S a m	Sam
t a n	tan

   Proceed to teach the sounds of all the letters in Lesson 1. These are: **t, m, h, f, d, w, g, l, c, s, and p.**

4. If a child is having difficulty remembering the sound of a letter, help him with an association such as:

s—"sss"—sound of a snake
m—"mmm"—when food tastes good
f—show picture of a fish
c—show picture of a cat
p—show picture of a pig
t—sound of a clock ticking
w—show picture of a wagon
n—sound made when saying "no"
h—laughing "ha ha"
d—show picture of a dog
g—show picture of a goat

All sounds can be associated with a picture or an act, and when the child forgets, e.g., **s**, say, "What does a snake say?" or "Remember the sound when you laugh?"

An additional procedure that is used for children who are hard to teach is to use the grapho-vocal method by having the child repeatedly write the letter, saying it at the same time. Repetition of writing and saying aids overlearning and decreases the child's tendency to forget. (See description of grapho-vocal method on page 00.)

Introducing Lesson 1. After the child has learned the short sound of the letter **a** and the sounds of some consonants, show the child how you want him to read the lessons. Sound out each word in the first line, one letter at a time, giving the complete word after sounding it. For example, read **"a t, at; s a t, sat; m a t, mat; h a t, hat; f a t, fat."** (Be sure to give the isolated sound of each letter and blend them smoothly. Guard against sounding letters like **h** and **b** as "huh" and "buh." If you are not used to sounding letters, practice with someone who is familiar with isolating the letter sounds and pronouncing them clearly and distinctly.)

Now ask the child to sound the letters in each word first; then say the word as you have demonstrated. If the child does not blend the sounds into a word automatically, it may be helpful to sound along with him, increasing the tempo so that he can hear the word when the sounds are closer together. If a child misreads a sound or forgets, prompt him by saying the correct sound. Continue to the end of the lesson.

Lessons 1 to 9 include the five vowels and all of the consonants. Continue with the lessons as fast as the child can learn them. By the end of Lesson 9, the child should be proficient in decoding words that include the short vowels and all the consonants. Sentences and stories introduced here remind the child that decoding aids in reading meaningful content.

Sometimes the child becomes fatigued in reading the lessons and begins to wander in attention or to make errors. At this point the teacher should use a segmented approach instead of the synthetic approach used in the lessons he has been having. Instead of asking him to synthesize sounds into words, ask him to break a word into its separate sounds or segments. Ask him to listen to the word **cap** or **top** or **nut** and tell you what the separate sounds are. What sound comes first? What sound is in the middle? What is the last sound? Require the child to sound each letter, write it, then say the word. Teaching the child to break up words into separate sounds and writing them gives him a new slant on blending and helps him to segment a word and put the pieces together again. The child can then return to the remedial lessons with renewed interest.

Organization of the Program

As has been noted before, only one new vowel sound is presented at a time. As each new sound is introduced, it is introduced in a variety of words so as to develop an automatic response to that particular symbol.

As new sound-symbol relationships are acquired, old ones are then reviewed along with the new one, again helping to imprint the sequence of sound-symbol associations.

Each lesson is organized into four parts. The first section of each lesson provides sequences of words in which only the initial consonant changes. This minimal change promotes errorless responding with all the words in each line rhyming.

In the second section of each lesson, the sequences of words again require only a minimal change, but here it is only the final consonant that changes. This change in pattern is necessary to avoid perseveration. Some children tend to develop a rhyming habit and do not isolate the vowel from the final consonant. This is used instead of the family system of phonics in which the **-at** family and the **-am** family are taught as units.

The third section increases the discriminative difficulty somewhat in that both initial and final consonants change.

The fourth section presents the same words but spaced normally instead of isolating each letter as they are in the first three sections.

Insofar as possible, the *Phonic Remedial Reading Lessons* have been sequenced from easy to difficult.

Part I presents single letters to be associated with single sounds. The nine lessons in this part include the short sounds of the five vowels, **a, o, i, u,** and **e,** with review lessons iterspersed to help imprint the several sound-symbol associations being learned.

Part II presents two- and three-letter sequences which have a single sound. The two-and three-letter symbols are written together, as in **d a sh, h ee l,** and **c a tch.** By writing these digraphs as units and spatially separating them from the other letters, they become a single configuration to be associated with a single sound, thus retaining the principle of one response to one symbol. Review lessons are also frequently introduced in Part II.

In *Part III* no new sound-symbol associations are introduced, but symbols already learned are clumped and integrated into larger units of graphemes such as consonant blends (**bl** as in **bl ock; spl** as in **spl it**) and common syllables (**unch** as in **l unch** or **p unch; ump** as in **j ump** or **p ump; est; ell; emp; ench**; etc.). This provides a "breathing space" in which the student may learn to perceive larger units and integrate sounds already learned.

Part IV presents new configurations which are more difficult or are larger units of graphemes such as **old** as in **c old, oll** as in **r oll, ook** as in **l ook, igh** as in **h igh** and **s ight.** Most of these make possible the decoding of words which are often taught as sight words but which have enough related words to form a category of words containing these sounds.

Part V presents some sounds which are exceptions to the sounds previously taught to certain configurations, such as the **ea** in **head**, the **ow** in **blow**, the long **o** sound at the end of a word as in **go** or **oe** as in **t oe.** At this more advanced level in the *Phonic Remedial Reading Lessons,* most students are capable of making choices and in using context clues.

Part VI merges into some grammatical understanding of plurals, possessives, past tense, present progressive, affixes, compound words, and syllabication.

Supplementary Remedial Procedures

Although there are numerous strategies that may be used to accompany the phonic lessons, only a few will be discussed below. These include (a) the grapho-vocal method, (b) teaching sight words and story reading, (c) selecting appropriate readers, and (d) tutoring children individually and in small groups.

The Grapho-Vocal Method

The term grapho-vocal is used here to mean the simultaneous use of motor and vocal responses of the child. In this strategy the child writes a letter and sounds it at the same time, or if a nonphonic word is targeted **(the, was)**, the child writes the word and says it at the same time. He thus sees it, writes it, says it, and hears it.

With children who can learn to read letter sounds and words rapidly, the grapho-vocal method may not be necessary. With children who have failed to read by the natural or sight method, the grapho-vocal method will be found to be helpful, and with children who are severely deficient, the procedure is absolutely necessary. The grapho-vocal strategy uses visual, motor, and verbal mediation strategies and is particularly useful with children who show marked reversal tendencies.

Sight Words and Short Stories

The *Phonic Remedial Reading Lessons* teach a process for decoding new words, i.e., giving clues for translating written language. This simplifies the reading process for those children who have had difficulty (a) in remembering unrelated new words, or (b) in generalizing their own methods of attacking new words. The *Phonic Remedial Reading Lessons* teach automatic responses to the written symbols, but since the English language is not completely phonetic, children must learn that there are some words they need to respond to as wholes. **The, is, go** are short words that children can recognize as complete sound units. This often requires specifically noting and practicing these words. For this reason, certain common nonphonic words are introduced in a supplementary ongoing program of consecutive reading using basically the phonic sounds and words just acquired. Sight words are printed in bold-type face to indicate that the child is not to sound them. Beginning with a few short sentences and later using story content, these exercises give the child a feeling of accomplishment in knowing that he is learning to read connected material with content.

Sight words and story content are used for only Part I and Part II. It has been found that with the basic sounds and a few nonphonic sight words included in the first two parts, children can now begin to use books. There are a number of books on the market, particularly some of the linguistic readers, that can now be used to increase the child's ability to read stories. It is suggested that in using readers, the teacher should first survey the story to be read and select the nonphonic words in the story that the child does not know. These words can be taught by using the grapho-vocal method. Require the child to read the stories, sound out the words the child does not yet know by sight, and prompt the child with non-phonic words, at the early stages. Accuracy and adequate decoding should be stressed. Time is not an element at the initial stages. Speed reading can be introduced later as the child acquires facility in reading.

The Use of Books

Different books should be used as soon as the child shows some facility in decoding words and in learning to recognize words as wholes. Some suggestions for selecting the right book to use are:

1. Find a book that is primarily phonetic. Many such books are available on the market. The linguistic readers are suitable since these include phonetic words.
2. For older children, select books that are more mature in content. An older child with a severe reading disability is insulted with primers and "baby books."
3. Avoid books with pictures. Pictures in a story become distractions from the task of paying attention to the printed symbols.
4. In reading a book, allow the child to sound the words that he can sound, but when he faces a word that does not correspond to the sounds which he has already learned, just tell the child the word and let him go on. Do the same for unfamiliar sight words. For example, if the child has not learned the word "who" but begins to sound it phonetically, just say "who." If, on the other hand, the child has forgotten a sound such as **oo** in "pool," point to the sound **oo** to aid the child in transferring the phonic lessons to sentence reading.
5. Keep a record of the words in a story that are frequently misread by the child and teach the child these words, by the grapho-vocal strategy if necessary.
6. Before the child reads a passage, call attention to the words in the passage that may be stumbling blocks. Point these out to the child and practice reading them. Words such as "where," "when," "their," "there," require additional exposure and practice.

Individual and Group Instruction

Although the *Phonic Remedial Reading Lessons* are described as an individual method for severe reading disabilities, successful treatment has been administered to two and three children at the same time. If a resource teacher has a number of children at the same level of reading ability, the following method is suggested:

1. Begin by giving individual instruction to the children for as many lessons as needed to get them functioning at the same level. This initial instruction should teach the children the prerequisite skills needed and the first lesson or two in the program. If two children are going to be taught together, they should be at the same skill level and should also be able to cooperate with each other and follow instructions.

2. Ask one child to read a line or two in a lesson, and ask the other child to say "stop" when the first child makes an error. Then alternate the reader and checker. Thus, as one child reads orally, the other child follows silently, saying "stop" each time the reader makes a mistake.

3. After the children have completed the lesson or a part of it, give both children paper and pencil and dictate words from the lesson. Require the children to use the grapho-vocal method. The children can then correct each other's words.

4. When stories are introduced, the same method as that used with the lessons may be employed. One child may read a passage orally while the other child reads silently and corrects errors.

It should be noted that some children cannot be taught in a group until they have reached a certain level of success and self-confidence. Either the child cannot be properly matched with some other child, or the child requires the complete attention of the teacher in a tutoring situation. Also, some children may react negatively to the competition inherent in this method. A resource teacher with a case load of 8 to 10 children can arrange to have such children taught in an individualized situation and others in groups of two and in some cases in groups of three. The ideal plan is to start a child in individual instruction, then in a group of two, and later when sufficient progress has been made, adjust the program in his regular class.

Recapitulation

The *Phonic Remedial Reading Lessons* are of value to severe reading disabled children (dyslexics) who require a systematic, step-by-step program of instruction. The suggestions for using the program are:

1. Prepare the child with the prerequisite skills of (a) visual and auditory discrimination, (b) sound blending, and (c) sound-symbol association of the short vowel **a** and some of the common consonants.

2. Always begin with Lesson 1 and proceed systematically to subsequent lessons. If an informal evaluation of a child indicates that he has adequate sound-blending ability and seems to learn sound-symbol associations readily, it is permissible to skip easy sections and go on to other lessons. Do not skip lessons, but if the program is moving too slowly for a particular child, administer part of the lesson to be certain the child knows the sounds. If, on the other hand, the child forgets the sounds of specific letters or does not readily decode the words when he sounds the separate parts, more time should be spent on sound-blending games and/or grapho-vocal exercises to imprint those specific sound-symbol associations. Try not to back-track in the lessons, but give informal experiences on the sounds he needs. Proceed in the lessons only as fast as the child can progress with success.

3. Require the child to sound each letter separately "out loud," even if he knows the

word by sight. Children with severe disabilities in decoding require this method to establish the habit of analyzing a word, sound by sound. It is necessary to overlearn the sounding habit. It will drop out at a later period when not needed. Research on learning has demonstrated that verbal mediation aids retention and recall. The *Phonic Remedial Reading Lessons* should always be conducted orally.

4. Stress accuracy rather than speed. Give the child plenty of time, but come to the rescue when needed to insure a correct response. Correct each error as it is made. If a child cannot recall a sound, prompt or say it for him, but return later to that sound for extra repetition. Make it easy for the child to know he is succeeding.

5. Use verbal praise frequently and freely. A child who has failed for years needs constant reinforcement. If he sounds out "**s a t**" and blends it into "**sat**," the teacher can say, "Yes, sat. That's good." By this confirmation the teacher reinforces the child.

6. Review lessons are important. These are introduced frequently for two reasons: (a) it gives the child more practice on specific sounds and in discriminating them from others, and (b) it tests the child's recall of sounds he has previously learned. If on the review lesson the child consistently makes errors on one sound in particular, the teacher can provide further experiences with that sound. Usually this can be done informally, but on occasion it may be necessary to extract parts of previous lessons.

7. Demand attention to the task and adhere to the lessons and stories. A remedial period is a period for intensive concentration and study. It should not be wasted on extraneous activities. The best procedure is to say to the child, "We are here to learn. Let's stick to the lessons." Short-term variations of the task, however, may sometimes be used to renew interest and challenge the child.

8. Use the segmental or analytic strategy. If a child becomes fatigued in reading the phonic lesson, stop and use the segmental strategy by asking the child to analyze words into their separate sounds. Teaching the child to break up words into separate sounds and writing them gives the child a new slant on sound blending and helps him to recognize the segments of a word and put the pieces together again. It is a helpful strategy to use when a child has difficulty in attending to the remedial exercises.

9. Nonphonic words are taught as word wholes. Such nonphonic words are introduced gradually in the stories that are interspersed among the remedial lessons. When they occur in the stories, the teacher is asked to initially just tell the child, "This word is 'the' (or 'is' or 'what'). Don't try to sound it. Just say, 'the' (or 'is' or 'what')." If the child does not recall the word after several occurrences, use the grapho-vocal method by having him copy the word, then erase it (or cover it) and try to write it from memory, saying the word as he writes it. This should be repeated several times.

10. Avoid teaching the rules of phonics. The lessons are so arranged that children learn to respond to a visual symbol automatically. Only later will they be helped to generalize similarities and differences on which the rules are based.

11. Teach nonphonic words by the grapho-vocal method. Generally, the child may learn nonphonic words when the teacher prompts him. If he fails to learn nonphonic sight words after several repetitions, use the grapho-vocal method.
12. Initially use books that rely heavily on phonic words. Among such books are many of the linguistic readers. Other books with a phonic emphasis are available.

PART 1

One Letter, One Sound

Lesson 1-A

a

a t	s a t	m a t	h a t	f a t
a m	h a m	S a m	P a m	t a m
s a d	m a d	h a d	l a d	d a d
w a g	s a g	t a g	l a g	h a g

s a t	s a p	S a m	s a d
m a p	m a m	m a d	m a t
h a g	h a m	h a t	h a d
c a t	c a p	c a d	c a m

s a t	a m	s a d	p a t	m a d
h a d	m a t	t a g	f a t	h a m
l a g	h a m	w a g	h a t	s a p
s a d	t a p	c a p	d a d	a t

map	hag	cat	sat	ham	tap
sap	map	hat	sad	tag	am
Pam	mat	had	tap	hat	dad
fat	mad	at	wag	cap	sag

To the teacher: This lesson introduces many of the consonant sounds. /b/, /r/, /n/, /j/, /x/, and /v/ are introduced in Lesson 1—B. The sounds of /y/, /z/, /k/, and /q/ are not introduced until still later.

Lesson 1-B

a

c a p   m a p   n a p   l a p   t a p

a n   v a n   c a n   m a n   f a n

a x   t a x   w a x   M a x   l a x

h a d   b a d   d a d   m a d   s a d

c a b   c a t   c a p   c a n

b a t   b a d   b a n   b a g

p a t   p a n   p a d   p a l

r a g   r a t   r a n   r a m

j a m   j a g   j a b   j a m

n a p   m a n   t a x   b a d   c a p

c a n   h a d   l a d   a x   r a n

t a p   w a x   m a d   f a n   a n

g a p   s a d   t a x   j a b   p a l

dad   van   cab   bat   dam   ram

bad   rat   ban   cap   wax   pad

fan   bag   pal   jam   tan   had

tax   map   ran   lap   gap   lad

Sam and Pam

Sam ran.

Pam ran.

Sam had jam.

Pam had jam.

Lesson 2

o

h o t   p o t   n o t   l o t   g o t
s o b   r o b   m o b   j o b   c o b
h o p   m o p   t o p   p o p   c o p
o x   b o x   f o x   l o x   p o x

p o p   p o d   p o t   p o d
c o d   c o p   c o t   c o g
r o b   r o d   r o t   r o b
m o m   m o p   m o b   m o m
j o g   j o b   j o t   j o b

d o t   c o b   c o t   g o t   p o t
t o p   r o t   m o b   j o t   m o p
j o b   t o t   h o p   p o d   j o g
r o b   c o b   p o p   o n   c o p
n o t   b o x   h o t   f o x   c o d

on   top   mob   not   rob   pot
mop   nod   hop   rod   sob   hot
lot   got   rob   pot   cod   dot
cop   ox   job   on   mom   rot

the

The Cop and the Mop

The cop can hop.

The cop can jog.

The cop can hop and jog.

The mop can not hop.

The mop can not jog.

To the teacher: Teach the word "the" as a sight word. See instructions for teaching sight words on page 16 of the directions.

Lesson 3 — Review

a and o

sat bag ham cap fad tan
jog on top got mob not
tag ran ham mop hot rod
lap man had rob hop dot

an on cat cot hot hat
pat pot rat rot mop map
pad pod cop cap top tap
ox ax sad sod pod pad

pot mad map at rot lad
mat mom cob dad tan Tom
nod jog fat yak nag cab
ran jot yam sob fan tax
rob bat sad pop lot and

box lot pal jog can pop nap pad
rob sat sob cot gap hot job cap
rod am got map wag on fan at
jam ham wax rag pod bad not and

a

Tom and the Pot

Tom had **a** pot.

The pot got hot.

Tom sat the pot on **a** box.

The pot and the box got hot.

Tom got mad at the pot.

To the teacher: Teach the word "a" as a sight word. See instructions for teaching sight word on page 16 of the directions.

Lesson 4

i

s i t	f i t	h i t	b i t	k i t
h i m	r i m	d i m	T i m	J i m
h i d	l i d	d i d	k i d	r i d
w i n	t i n	s i n	f i n	b i n
w i ll	f i ll	p i ll	t i ll	h i ll

h i t	h i m	h i d	h i p
s i n	s i t	s i p	s i x
r i b	r i m	r i p	r i g
p i g	p i n	p i t	p i g

r i g	l i d	t i n	r i m	f i t
s i p	p i g	r i b	s i t	h i t
h i m	s i n	l i p	p i n	h i d
f i x	p i g	h i p	s i x	f i ll
i n	t i p	r i m	d i g	z i p

kit	Bill	fin	nip	dim	it	miss
Tim	rid	lip	sin	hit	hip	if
dip	win	Jim	pig	zip	him	fit
dig	big	fill	rib	six	bit	in
kid	six	tip	rim	sit	bid	fib

The Pig Got Hit

A kid had a fat pig.

The pig got hit.

A cab hit the pig.

The cab hit the pig in the rib.

The cab did not kill the pig.

Lesson 5 — Review

a o i

sat cap rag can sad mat
not sob hop rod cop pot
sit him sip win fig hid
cap cop sit sat hop hip
tip tap pot pat hid had

hat hot hit pot pit pat
tip tap top sop sip sap
lop lip lap had hod hid
on in an at it if

fit cat dot cop lap sip
rag fig rob sip mad sob
pod rip fat sag mix hot
bag pot jog nip fig man
hip cob fan did mob cab
six rod wag kit got map

pan sad lot pit jog six rip ran
rat yam dot Sam pop can kid gap
sad big wag fin nod tin dig top
Jim tan sop sit mob dam cot zip

is

Pam Can Hit It

Hit it Pam.

Hit it in the box.

If the box **is** big, Pam can hit it in.

If the box **is** not big, Pam can not hit it in.

The box **is** big and Pam can hit it in.

To the teacher: Teach the word "is" as a sight word. See instructions for teaching sight words on page 16 of the directions.

Lesson 6

u

n u t   h u t   c u t   b u t   r u t
  f u n   r u n   s u n   g u n   b u n
r u g   m u g   t u g   j u g   d u g
  h u b   r u b   t u b   s u b   p u b

h u t   h u m   h u g   h u b
  r u n   r u g   r u b   r u m
b u s   b u zz   b u g   b u n
  s u n   s u m   s u p   s u b
c u t   c u p   c u b   c u d

c u p   f u n   h u b   s u m   r u g
  h u t   r u n   b u s   c u t   u s
n u n   f u zz   b u d   r u g   h u m
  m u d   j u g   s u b   c u b   r u n
s u b   u p   t u b   g u m   t u g

hut   mud   hug   rub   sun   sum
  us   dug   jut   tug   gun   bun
tub   up   cut   sun   pub   mud
  but   sub   gut   dud   buzz   bug

The Man and the Bug

The bus ran up the hill.

A man got on the bus.

A bug got on the bus.

The bug did buzz and the man did hum.

The bug bit the man and the man hit the bug.

The bug did not buzz, but the man did hum.

Lesson 7—Review

a o i u

pad fat gap jam nap pan
tin fib pig lid bit him
dot mop Tom cob jog pop
cup fun hub sum rug bud

tub tab mud mad bud bad
cub cab rub rib nut not
fizz fuzz dug dig in on
big bag bug cat cot cut
hit hot hut sap sup sip
rum ram rim jug jog jig
bit bat but hum him ham

pot in us top nut cob
sad bud dim rug dam hit
got dad bun nap gum mud
am dot mop tin up fun
fib sip sum cob rug pop

fill hag bat will bun cot pit six
top mob tan tub jog hid rip bat
nod wag him dug pup dot hip dad
fix Bob man hiss rod up sop miss

is his as has

Bud Has a Pup

Bud **has** a big pup.

His pup is not **as** big **as** a pig, but it **is as** big **as** a cub.

The big pup dug in the mud.

Bud **is** mad at **his** pup, and **his** pup **is** sad.

The pup **has** mud on it.

The pup can not sit on **his** lap.

The pup did hop on the rug.

The rug **has** mud on it.

To the teacher: Teach the words "is," "his," "as," and "has" as sight words. See instructions for teaching sight words on page 16 of the directions.

Lesson 8

e

b e t　　n e t　　g e t　　p e t　　s e t
j e t　　w e t　　v e t　　y e t　　l e t
d e n　　h e n　　m e n　　p e n　　t e n
b e g　　k e g　　l e g　　p e g　　M e g
b e d　　f e d　　l e d　　w e d　　r e d
f e ll　　w e ll　　b e ll　　s e ll　　t e ll

b e t　　b e g　　b e d　　b e t
m e t　　m e n　　M e g　　m e n
p e t　　p e n　　p e g　　p e p
l e t　　l e g　　l e d　　l e ss
y e t　　y e s　　y e ll　　y e p

b e t　　d e n　　b e ll　　b e d　　n e t
p e n　　w e d　　b e g　　h e n　　j e t
w e t　　m e n　　n e t　　l e g　　f e d
r e d　　m e t　　p e g　　t e n　　l e t
w e t　　y e s　　y e t　　b e t　　p e p

net　jet　fed　get　ten　wed　set　led
hen　bed　keg　net　set　peg　leg　den
mess　vet　pen　wed　men　bet　get　ten
wet　red　pet　yes　less　set　wet　yet

?

Questions and Answers

Is the red hen wet?

Yes, the red hen is wet.

Can the men get fed?

Yes, the men can get fed.

Did the vet sell a pet?

Yes, the vet did sell a pet.

Can Meg sell us a pen?

Yes, Meg can sell us a pen.

To the teacher: Teach the meaning of a question mark before having the children read the sentences containing question marks.

Lesson 9 — Review

a u o e i

m a t   c a n   w a g   c o g   n o d   g o t
t i n   f i b   p i g   s i x   b i t   r i p
r u n   t u b   f u n   b u t   s u n   b u zz
p e n   p e t   y e s   m e n   r e d   t e n

p e t   p o t   g e t   g o t   l o t   l e t
r e d   r o d   n o d   N e d   p e p   p o p
n e t   n u t   b u t   b e t   B e n   b u n
p e p   p u p   b u d   b e d   b e g   b u g
p i n   p e n   b i t   b e t   w e t   w i t

m e ss   f e ll   b a d   b u m   j o t   d i n
w i n   m e t   g u n   f a t   y e s   r a t
g e t   s a t   l o t   m e n   s i p   t u g
t e n   c a n   s i t   r u n   l e g   h a g

six   man   men   cot   cut   yet   bat   beg
met   but   get   got   hut   ran   top   gum
pep   hat   peg   not   wig   pen   pin   hid
rot   ten   hen   tin   led   bet   cot   wet

to

Meg Gets a Pet

Dad and Mom and Meg ran **to** the vet **to** get a pet.

Meg did not get a pup.

Meg did not get a pig.

Meg did not get a red hen.

The vet did sell a big cat **to** Meg.

Meg got a box **to** fit the cat.

The cat had a big mat **to** nap on.

The cat has not wet the mat yet.

To the teacher: Teach the word "to" as a sight word. See instructions for teaching sight words on page 16 of the directions.

Test for Part I

* *To the teacher:* This test contains all the sounds taught in Part I. If the child makes two errors out of three on any vowel, reteach that vowel sound.

sad
red
gun
tin
hot
top
ran
cut
men
pig
sun
pat
fit
set
rob

PART II

Two or More Letters, One Sound

Lesson 10

sh

d a sh	c a sh	g a sh	l a sh
m a sh	r a sh	s a sh	d a sh
d i sh	f i sh	w i sh	d i sh
g u sh	m u sh	h u sh	r u sh

sh u t	sh u n	sh u sh	sh u t
sh e d	sh e ll	sh e d	sh e ll
sh o p	sh o t	sh o d	sh o p
sh a g	sh a m	sh a d	sh a ll

d a sh	sh i p	m a sh	sh o d
sh o p	d i sh	g u sh	sh e ll
c a sh	sh i n	r a sh	sh o t
f i sh	m u sh	sh u sh	r u sh
sh u n	s a sh	sh o p	w i sh

shad	shod	cash	fish	rush	sham
dash	shun	dish	mush	sash	shell
ship	gush	rash	shed	lash	shop
mash	shut	gash	shall	wish	cash

The Big Fish

A big fish is at the dam. A kid will dash to the dam to get the fish. But the kid can not get the fish. If the kid can dash to the ship, the kid can get the fish. The kid fell in the sand. The kid got a shell, but not the fish.

Lesson 11

ch tch

m u ch   s u ch   D u tch   h u tch   m u ch
i tch   w i tch   p i tch   h i tch   d i tch
h a tch   c a tch   m a tch   l a tch   p a tch

ch a p   ch a t   ch a p   ch a ff
ch i n   ch i p   ch i ll   ch i n
ch u g   ch u m   ch u g   ch u b

r i ch   ch a p   h a tch   ch i n   d i tch
m u ch   p i tch   ch a t   c a tch   ch i p
p a tch   ch u g   h i tch   m u ch   m a tch
ch i ll   r i ch   ch o p   i tch   ch u m
l a tch   ch o p   p a tch   ch i n   ch u g

batch   rich   chess   chap   such   chill
latch   chop   chum   pitch   chug   hatch
chat   chin   hitch   patch   chop   catch
much   itch   chin   ditch   chum   chip

of

The Mud Patch

Dan has a chum. The chum **of** Dan ran to a patch **of** grass. His chum fell in a ditch. The ditch had a lot **of** mud in it. His chum had a bunch **of** mud on his chin. His chum had such an itch. The chum **of** Dan is a sad chap.

Lesson 12

ck

b a ck	s a ck	sh a ck	p a ck	t a ck
p i ck	s i ck	N i ck	k i ck	l i ck
r o ck	s o ck	d o ck	sh o ck	l o ck
t u ck	l u ck	b u ck	d u ck	m u ck
p e ck	ch e ck	n e ck	d e ck	b e ck

p i ck	p e ck	p a ck	p u ck
r o ck	r a ck	R i ck	r u ck
d u ck	d o ck	d e ck	D i ck
l o ck	l a ck	l u ck	l i ck

w i ck	w i tch	p i t	p i tch
h a t	h a tch	p a ck	p a tch
s i ck	s a ck	s t i tch	s t i ck
l a tch	l a ck	R i ck	r i ch
b a ck	b a tch	l i ck	l u ck
D u tch	d u ck	s h ock	s o ck

kick	chick	suck	luck	tick	check
Dick	puck	wick	check	sock	catch
buck	block	shock	chuck	shack	peck
muck	neck	rock	peck	lock	buck

At the Duck Camp

Rick and Dick went to a camp. At the camp Dick had a bit of luck. Dick shot a duck in the neck. Rick had a lot of luck. Rick shot a big duck and sat it on the rim of the dock. Dick had to check on the ducks and fit the ducks in a sack.

Lesson 13

oo

z oo   m oo   t oo   b oo
b oo t   sh oo t   r oo t   l oo t
l oo n   m oo n   s oo n   n oo n
c oo l   f oo l   t oo l   p oo l

r oo t   r oo m   r oo f   r oo t
b oo   b oo m   b oo t   b oo n
m oo n   m oo d   m oo t   m oo r
h oo t   h oo f   h oo p   h oo t

b oo t   m oo n   c oo l   r oo m   f oo d
r oo f   h oo p   b oo n   z oo   f oo l
sh oo t   m oo d   l oo p   r oo t   p oo r
s oo n   t oo l   b oo   m oo n   b oo m

roof   boot   hoop   soon   toot   moon
hoop   mood   tool   shoot   cool   boom
hoof   loot   noon   fool   room   loop
pool   zoo   food   root   moor   too

was **were**

At the Zoo

The zoo **was** shut at noon. It **was** cool and lush in the zoo. At noon the big cats **were** fed milk to sip and food to sup on. To get the food to the cats, a man **was** let in to the zoo. The man set the dish in the pen. Soon the cats **were** fed. The pigs **were** fed too.

Lesson 14

ee ea

b ee   s ee   f ee   t ee   l ee
s ee k   w ee k   p ee k   ch ee k   m ee k
w ee p   k ee p   d ee p   s ee p   sh ee p

b ee   b ee f   b ee t   b ee ch   b ee p
s ee   s ee n   s ee d   s ee m   s ee p
w ee   w ee p   w ee d   w ee k   w ee p

ea t   s ea t   h ea t   n ea t   m ea t
h ea p   ch ea p   l ea p   r ea p   h ea p
ea ch   t ea ch   b ea ch   r ea ch   p ea ch

b ea t   b ea n   b ea m   b ea k   b ea d
l ea k   l ea d   l ea f   l ea n   l ea p
r ea d   r ea l   r ea m   r ea p   r ea ch

f ee l   s ea t   r ea d   f ee d   ea t   l ea f
b ee t   l ea p   m ea n   b ee   p ea ch   w ee p
s ea m   h ee l   n ee d   sh ee t   ch ea t   sh ee p

need   meal   bee   seek   read   cheat   meet
mean   team   seam   beet   leap   meet   see
heel   sea   see   bead   peek   meat   feet
sheet   peal   bean   reap   mean   dean   seep

he she we me be

A Bee is a Bee

A bee is a bee.
And I am **me.**

I am **me.**
Not **he** or **she.**
I am just **me.**

We will let Bill **be** Bill.
He is **he.**

We will let Dee **be** Dee.
She is **she.**

We can let a bee **be** a bee.
But let **me be me.**

Let **me be me.**
And **we** will see
If I can **be**
The best I can **be.**

Lesson 15

oa

oa t	b oa t	c oa t	g oa t		
r oa d	t oa d	l oa d	g oa d		
c oa s t	r oa s t	b oa s t	t oa s t		
c oa t	c oa l	c oa x	c oa ch		
r oa d	r oa m	r oa ch	r oa s t		
l oa n	l oa d	l oa m	l oa f		
b oa t	b a t	c a t	c oa t	g o t	g oa t
c oa ch	c a tch	m oa n	m a n	g oa l	g a l
s o ck	s oa k	m a t	m oa t	s oa p	s a p
l a d	l oa d	r o d	r oa d	c o t	c oa t
load	goat	moan	soak	boat	poach
coat	oat	roach	road	oak	goad
load	coach	coax	soap	soak	roam
oak	toast	moat	loaf	boast	roast

you I

Fun at the Beach

You and **I** went to the beach. It is fun to be at the beach. **I** float in the sea. **You** sit in a boat as it floats. We run in the hot sand and get hot feet, as hot as coals. Then we soak in the sea to get cool. **You** and **I** can be real pals.

I left my red coat at the beach. **I** left it in a black oak boat. **You** got the coat, but it got wet in the mud. We will soak the coat, but we will need soap to get it clean. If **I** get in a boat, my coat will not be in the boat.

Lesson 16 – Review

sh oo ch ee ck oa
tch ea

c a sh   sh o p   f i sh   sh e ll   r u sh   w i sh
f oo d   l oo m   p oo l   b oo t   sh oo t   m oo n
ch u g   m a tch   ch o p   s u ch   ch i ll   i tch
s ee   ea t   m ea t   b ee t   sh ee t   d ea l
b a ck   p i ck   l o ck   p u ck   ch u ck   sh a ck
l oa d   oa t   s oak   c oa ch   r oa m   c oa t

c a sh   c a tch   ch i p   sh i p   d i sh   d i tch
m a tch   m a sh   sh i n   ch i n   l u sh   l u ck
p i ck   p i tch   w i tch   w i ck   b a ck   b a tch
m u ck   m u ch   m u sh   sh u sh   s u ch   s u ck
b oo t   b oa t   m oa n   m oo n   c oo l   c oa l
r oo m   r oa m   f oo l   f oa l   l oo m   l oa m

s ee d   f i sh   s oa k   l o ck   c oa ch   sh ee t
ch ea t   m ee t   z oo   m u ch   p i tch   b a ck
l a sh   ch u m   s a ck   m a tch   b oa s t   i tch
sh oo t   s oo n   r oa ch   ch ee k   sh a ck   oa k

sack   wish   chuck   hitch   foam   loot
shoot   meat   cheek   poach   cheap   too
soak   shoo   luck   latch   road   dock
shack   patch   mash   reach   coach   zoo

We Plant Seeds

I will dig a plot for seeds. You can weed the plot. We will get food to eat from the plot. We will plant pea seeds and beet seeds. Dad will plant a peach seed. It will be a tree. He will pick each peach and chill it and peel it.

We will mash the peas on a dish to feed a wee tot. She will be glad to eat the peas. If she is not neat, she will get peas on her cheek and chin.

Lesson 17

th wh

th a n	th a t	th i s	th ee
th e m	th e n	th a n	th u s
wh i p	wh i ch	wh i m	wh i t
wh ea t	wh ee l	wh a ck	wh a m
wh e n	wh e t	wh i s t	wh i ch
wh e n	th e n	th e m	th u s
wh ea t	th ee	wh ee l	wh i s t
wh i p	th a t	wh a m	th i s
th a n	wh a ck	wh e t	wh i t

than	whack	wheel	then	thus
whist	which	than	that	wheat
whip	them	thus	which	wheel
whim	whip	them	this	whack

there **where**

Where is the whip?

The whip is on that rock.

Will **there** be food **there**?

Yes, **there** will be food **there.**

Which wheel is that on?

It is on my wheel.

Is that wheat **there** to eat?

Yes, that wheat is **there** to eat.

When will this meat get **there**?

It will get **there** when it is ten.

Which kid is less than six?

That kid **there** is less than six.

Which man will tell them **where** to sleep?

This man will tell them **where** to sleep.

Lesson 18

aw au

j aw	p aw	r aw	s aw
th aw	l aw	sh aw l	c r aw l
p aw n	l aw n	d aw n	f aw n

P au l	h au l	m au l	S au l
l au d	M au d	f r au d	d au b
t au n t	h au n t	g au n t	

p aw	d au b	l aw	l aw n	l au n ch
h aw k	h au l	h au n t	f l aw	f r au d
p aw	j aw	sh aw l	m au l	g au n t

raw	maul	draw	fraud	crawl	Paul
gaunt	saw	law	hawk	haunt	flaw
laud	lawn	pawn	flaw	Maud	launch

little

The Sad **Little** Fawn

Maud and Paul saw a **little** fawn on the lawn near the shed. A truck had hit the **little** beast and it did not run. It had to crawl. Its hip was weak and limp. On its jaw the fawn had a raw gash. What a sad **little** fawn!

Paul had to lift the fawn and haul it into the shed to let Maud patch it up. Paul went to get a cup of milk, and Maud fed it to the sick fawn. Then the **little** fawn went to sleep and got well.

Lesson 19

-ng
ing, ang, ung, ong

s ing   w ing   k ing   th ing   r ing
s ang   b ang   r ang   h ang   g ang
r ung   s ung   l ung   h ung   s t ung
s ong   l ong   g ong   p r ong   s t r ong

s ing   s ang   s ung   r ing   r ang   r ung
c l ing   c l ung   h ang   h ung   l ong   l ung
s t ing   s t ung   f l ing   f l ung   s t r ong   s t r ung

fish ing   kick ing   pick ing   stick ing
match ing   fool ing   boat ing   back ing
cheer ing   load ing   feel ing   weep ing
sing ing   wing ing   bring ing   sting ing
hang ing   gang ing   long ing   bang ing

lung   sing   hang   hung   long   bang
clung   thing   swung   song   rang   stung
gang   singing   gong   banging   boating   keeping
hushing   song   rung   wishing   hung   sting
fussing   rushing   lung   fang   strong   catching

what

What is it?

What is that thing hanging on the long stick? Is it a fish? Is it a ring? Is it strong? Is it a bat? Has it hung on long? **What** can it be?

It seems to me it is too long to be a fish. It is too big to be a ring. It is not singing. It is not kicking. It is ringing.

What is it? It must be a bell.

Lesson 20

-nk
ank, ink, unk

b ank	b l ank	r ank	s ank	s p ank
t ank	c r ank	p r ank	sh ank	p l ank

ink	th ink	w ink	l ink	m ink
p ink	s ink	s t ink	b l ink	c l ink

j unk	b unk	h unk	ch unk	s unk
d unk	f l unk	p unk	s t unk	s k unk

s ink	s unk	b l ink	b l ank	p ink	p unk
c l ink	c l ank	c l unk	s t ink	s t ank	s t unk
b ank	b unk	r ink	r ank	th ink	th ank

tank	junk	pink	ink	bank	dunk
spank	bunk	flunk	sink	skunk	hunk
punk	prank	stink	wink	shank	drunk
sunk	flank	clink	stink	link	drank

said

What Stunk?

A little skunk sat on a stump.

The stump **said** that the skunk stunk.

But the skunk **said** that the stump stunk.

Did the skunk stink?

Or did the stump stink?

Did the stump or the skunk stink?

What did each think?

Lesson 21

ew ue

n ew f ew ch ew y ew L ew
b l ew s l ew f l ew s t ew s t r ew
b r ew d r ew g r ew th r ew c r ew

S ue d ue r ue t r ue c l ue
f l ue b l ue g l ue h ue t r ue

b l ew b l ue b r ew f l ew f l ue
g l ue sh r ew sh r ew d ch ew t r ue
c l ue d r ew th r ew s t ew b r ew
d ue d ew s c r ew c r ew d r ew

blue crew new brew hue clue
flew drew blew clue blue Lew
stew glue grew screw true clue
flue due crew shrewd dew crew
newt lewd true sued glued flue

bird

Lew and the Little **Bird**

Lew had a fear of **birds.** When a little blue **bird** fell out of its nest, she landed near a yew tree. The little **bird** just lay near there and went "peep, peep." Lew threw **bird** seed at the little blue **bird** for her to eat. "There you are, little **bird**," said Lew.

But the Mama blue **bird** did not like what she saw. She was a shrewd **bird**. She did not like it when Lew threw things at the little blue **bird**. She flew from her nest. She flew at Lew and came near to him with her big beak.

Poor Lew! Was the **bird** going to chew him up? He drew back and began to sob. "What shall I do? What shall I do?" he said as he ran home. That gave Lew a fear of **birds** from then on.

Lesson 22

Long Vowels with Final -e

a o

ate	d ate	r ate	g ate	f ate	
c ase	c ame	c ake	c ane	c ave	
ape	s ame	s ale	f ame	t ape	
f ate	m ade	p ale	m ane	g ame	

cap	cape	mat	mate	hat	hate
pal	pale	can	cane	pan	pane
mad	made	fat	fate	rat	rate

h ope	m ope	d ope	r ope	c ope
d ome	d ose	d ove	d oze	d ole
c ode	h ome	t ote	b one	c one
r ode	m ope	sh one	c ove	p oke

mop	mope	note	not	dote	dot
rod	rode	rot	rote	cod	code
hope	hop	tot	tote	tone	ton

male	mole	sale	sole	rate	rote
cake	coke	doze	daze	pale	pole
cave	cove	made	mode	dome	dame

make	sole	poke	sale	lane	code
mope	rate	shone	ate	choke	tone
joke	shame	rope	shade	cope	maze
pane	late	hope	fame	cave	dole

no go so

Can a gate run?
No, a gate can not run.

Can an ape **go** fast?
Yes, an ape can **go** fast.

Can a pole swim?
No, a pole can not swim.

Is a cap a cape?
No, a cap is not a cape.

Can a cap **go** with a cape?
Yes, a cap can **go** with a cape.

Is a cod a code?
No, a cod is not a code.

Can a plum **go** with a date?
Yes, you eat a plum and a date.

Did Sid bake a cake?
Yes, Sid did bake a cake.

Is this a note?
No, this is not a note.
It is a nut, **so** you can eat it.

Did he shave?
Yes, he did shave **so** he can **go**.

Lesson 23

Long Vowels with Final -e
i u

f ine	w ine	d ine	sh ine	l ine	
m ine	m ite	M ike	m ile	s m ile	
f ile	l ine	k ite	p ipe	b ite	
p ine	h ide	d ike	w ide	p ile	
rip	ripe	hide	hid	fin	fine
bit	bite	sit	site	pine	pin
dim	dime	kit	kite	wine	win
d uke	j uke	n uke	L uke	f l uke	
d une	d ude	d upe	d uke	r ule	
r ude	j ute	d ude	n ude	l ube	
l ure	t ube	l ute	J une	f l ute	
jut	jute	tub	tube	dud	dude
plum	plume	crud	crude	dune	dun
duke	dike	Luke	like	dine	dune
rude	ride	rope	ripe	dupe	dope
mile	male	prude	pride	lute	late
dune	mine	lure	tune	tide	pike
prude	time	shine	rule	hide	dude
smile	pine	tube	flute	line	pipe
dime	duke	June	bite	bike	nuke

The Bike Ride

As we went home, Mike gave me a ride on his fine red bike. When we went past the lake we met Luke and his bride. She sat with Luke on his bike.

Just then the dike broke and Luke and his bride and the bike slid into the lake. Luke was hit on his chin and neck with the bike and was just floating. His bride was real wet. Mike, as brave as he was, ran into the lake to save Luke and his bride and the bike too. The bride gave Mike a big hug and a smile to thank him. Mike did like that. It did make him feel like a duke.

Lesson 24 – Review

th aw -ng -nk ew (Long Vowels)
wh au ue

th at	th e n	th u s	th e m	th a n	th i s
wh i ch	wh a ck	wh ea t	wh i p	wh ee l	wh i z
s aw	r aw	c r aw l	l aw n	c l aw	sh aw l
h au l	P au l	M au d	h au n t	f r au d	d au b
r ang	w ing	l ong	s ong	s ung	l ung
ink	s ink	b ank	s ank	j unk	s unk
t ape	s ale	g ame	h ope	r obe	h ome
w ine	m ile	l ine	j uke	n ude	t ube
th en	wh e n	th ee	wh ee	th e m	wh i m
w ink	w ing	b ang	b ank	s ink	s ing
d ime	d ame	d ome	m ile	m ale	m ole
t ome	t ame	t ime	Sh ane	sh ine	sh one
th i s	wh a m	wh ile	th e n	d ope	wh ea t
catch ing	b ang	fish ing	s t ing	f ine	wh e n
t ube	p ipe	d ine	th a t	g ave	c l ing
w ink	s ank	b one	t ime	th e n	keep ing
sank	while	when	blue	haul	draw
choke	five	fluke	whip	this	dupe
shocking	role	ticking	cave	made	joke
sale	banging	sunk	them	lawn	shawl

The Winning Ring

The king was to give a ring to the man that was as strong as he was. Dave had the hope to win the ring, but he was not strong. Dave did go to the king. He said: "I am not strong, but I can sing a tune and make a song on the flute. It will make you smile for a long time. Can I win the ring?"

The king said yes. So then, Dave sang for a long time. That made the king smile wide. The king said: "Dave, there is some fine wine you can drink. You were not as strong as I, but you did make me feel fine. So you can have this ring." Fame came to Dave when he got that ring.

Lesson 25

ar

t ar	f ar	j ar	b ar
c ar t	p ar t	d ar t	ch ar t
c ar d	y ar d	h ar d	l ar d
f ar m	h ar m	ch ar m	ar m

ar ch	ar k	ar m	ar t
h ar d	h ar k	h ar m	h ar p
b ar	b ar d	b ar k	b ar n
m ar k	m ar ch	m ar sh	m ar t

b ar	c ar t	y ar n	ar m	c ar d
ar k	b ar n	y ar d	m ar k	d ar k
d ar n	t ar	m ar ch	ch ar m	d ar k
h ar p	m ar t	c ar d	sh ar k	p ar t

chart	lard	mark	sharp	farm	shark
part	car	harp	charm	dark	hard
far	marsh	lark	bark	card	darn
dart	yard	mart	arm	harm	march

they

Carl and Barbara

Carl was a singing bard from a far land. He came to a park to sing to kids. **They** did like him a lot. Carl had a sad life so he sang sweet songs for fun.

In March, he met Barbara at the park. She was from a farm. She came to the park three times a week to sell her art. She was an artist.

The last time Barbara came to the park a mean gang of men spat on her art. Then **they** darted into a barn. Carl ran to the barn. **They** ran fast, but Carl got them. He said, "Get going—go, go go!" Then the three men ran from the park. **They** did not harm her art.

Carl and Barbara loaded the art on the cart. **They** drove to Barbara's home on the farm. The next time Carl was free he went back to the farm to sing to Barbara. And the next time and the next time and the next time he went too.

Lesson 26

or

b or n	c or n	h or n	t or n	w or n
s or t	f or t	p or t	sh or t	n or th
f or k	p or k	c or k	c or d	l or d
or	n or	f or	f or d	f or m

h or n	p or t	c or k	f or m	f or
sh or t	t or n	c or d	n or	b or n
w or n	l or d	f or k	f or d	sh or t
w ore	b or n	s or t	n or th	h or n

for	far	form	farm	barn	born
cord	card	port	part	tort	tart
lard	lord	tar	torn	porch	parch
ore	are	card	cord	pork	park

corn	fort	pork	or	north	wore
born	cork	port	horn	nor	form
bore	sort	tore	worn	porch	short
sore	form	torn	fork	more	shore

have

The Scare Cora Had

Cora went to Fort Ord to see Nora and **have** fun with her. They did not need much cash, for it was fun to just march arm in arm from street to street to see what sort of morning it was.

On this morning the sun was just starting to come up and the grass was still wet. Cora and Nora started to go north from Nora's home. At the corner, Cora darted in to the street. What a scare she had! A horn tooted and she had to stop short. Nora had to grab Cora's dress to get her back from the street.

"Let's **have** more care," said Nora. "That car just missed you. Let's go rest on the next porch." As she got up on the porch, Cora saw that the short dress she wore was torn. "I **have** a torn dress. You tore this dress, Nora!"

"What if I did? It is better than getting hit! I **have** a clean dress for you at home. Let's go."

Lesson 27

ay ai

s ay	d ay	h ay	l ay	r ay
b ay	m ay	p ay	j ay	w ay
g r ay	p r ay	s p r ay	f r ay	b r ay
l ay	p l ay	c l ay	s l ay	p l ay

n ai l	s ai l	j ai l	t ai l	p ai l
m ai n	r ai n	ch ai n	p ai n	g ai n
p ai d	m ai d	l ai d	r ai d	s t ai d
r ai d	b r ai d	b r ai n	r ai n	r ai l

s ai l	p r ay	r ai n	ch ai n	s t ay
d ay	m ai l	s p r ay	m ai m	m ai l
g r ay	G ai l	s l ay	g ai n	g ay
c l ay	p r ay	p l ay	w ai t	p ai n t

bait	may	tail	stay	sail	jail
say	laid	play	raid	chain	pray
main	day	wait	bray	mail	sail
jay	paid	fray	train	gray	gay

one once

The Train

One day in May the train was late. Gail and Ray had to wait a long time for the train. They were waiting for the mail that the train was bringing.

Three kids were playing on the train tracks. **One** kid was standing on the rail and went step, step, step on the rail. Can he still stay on? He fell off just **once.**

Soon the long, gray train came sailing along as if it had wings or sails. It was going so fast to gain the time it had lost. At **one** time it was made late when a bad rain storm made a shack tip on to the train tracks. The junk had to stay on the tracks until the men had time to take the boards and nails and things off the tracks.

"Toot! Toot! Toot!" came the train. Pray that the kids get off the rails. Then **one** railroad man ran yelling at the kids. "Get off! Get off! The train is here." Gail and Ray felt glad that not **one** of the kids was on the tracks too long. They were glad to pick up the mail and soon be on the way home.

Lesson 28

ou ow qu

ou ch c ou ch p ou ch g r ou ch c r ou ch
out shout pout spout scout
f ou n d r ou n d h ou n d p ou n d s ou n d

c ow h ow n ow p l ow b ow
ow l f ow l h ow l p r ow l g r ow l
g ow n d ow n t ow n b r ow n c l ow n

qu i ck qu i z qu i t qu i ll qu i l t
qu e s t qu e ll qu a ck qu ake qu e n ch
qu ai l qu i p qu i ck qu ee n qu ee r

ou t h ow t ow n qu i z sh ou t qu i ck
br ow n f ou n d qu i t d ow n qu ai l c ou ch
p l ow n ou n qu ake r ou n d qu i ll b ow

ouch owl quit queen out quick
clown couch how quail crown now
noun quack hound pout plow brown
round quiz mouth grouch gown quilt

are

The Hound and the Owl

Once upon a time a lone queen had a home in a green forest. She had a queer hound for a pet. He was prowling around the yard much of the time. The queen made him bark and howl at things that came near. She said: "You **are** a pet of mine. You **are** to howl. You **are** to bark at things that **are** near me."

The next day a quail and an owl came into the yard and sat on the grass. The hound gave a quick, loud bark and started to growl. "You **are** to go away," the hound said. "Go away!" The quail was quick to run into the forest, but the owl just sat on the grass.

The hound said to himself, "I will get that owl!" He ran at the owl with a big, wide mouth, barking and growling. But the owl just said, "Hoot-hoot-hoo," and went up into a tree. The hound kept on barking until the queen came out to see what was the matter. She said: "You **are** a real loud hound. What is the matter?"

"Those birds were in the yard," said the hound. "The quail went away, but there is the owl up in the tree."

The queen had to tell the hound that owls were not bad. "You **are** foolish to bark at an owl. You **are** not smart to make an owl mad."

The owl just said, "Hoot-hoot-hoo!"

Lesson 29

er ir ur

h er	h er d	H er b	v er b	j er k
p er	p er m	p er t	p er k	p er ch
f ir	s ir	s t ir	sh ir t	d ir t
f ir s t	f ir m	f l ir t	b ir d	g ir l
h ur t	B ur t	b l ur t	c ur t	s p ur t
c ur	c ur b	c ur t	c ur l	ch ur ch
f er n	p er t	l ur k	h er d	b ur n
c ur l	b ur p	b ir ch	f ir m	b ir d
v er b	g ir l	h ur t	p er ch	ch ur ch
d ir t	h er	s ir	sh ir t	f ur

lurk	birch	bird	turn	her	curb
jerk	hurl	perch	dirt	sir	fur
whirl	fern	curl	hurt	girl	church
herd	chirp	turn	verb	curb	shirt

come **some**

The Store is on Fire

The store is burning. The store is on fire. When will the fire truck **come**? Get **some** hose. Where is the hose? It is under the steps.

Bert said to the girl, "Turn on the hose. Be fast."

The girl said, "Go to the church next to us. There is **some** water there. We will form a bucket line. Get a lot of pails and buckets and a lot of helpers." The first man fills a pail and hands it to the next man. He hands it to the man on the curb, where the man on the curb hands it to the next man, and on to the next and the next until the pail gets to the fire. One more pail, five more, ten more, twenty. No one shirks on the job. The water keeps going from man to man and is dumped on the fire. There! The fire is going out.

Bert gave the hose a jerk and it began to spurt **some** water on the fire. There it **comes**. The fire is out. The shirts and skirts did not burn, and no one got hurt. The bird on his perch up there in the birch tree began to chirp. He is glad, too, that no one got hurt.

Lesson 30

oy oi

t oy b oy j oy R oy s oy
c oy c l oy p l oy B oy d T r oy

oi l b oi l c oi l t oi l s oi l
f oi l b oi l b r oi l s oi l s p oi l
c oi n l oi n j oi n j oi n t p oi n t

b oy b oi l R oy t oi l t oy
b r oi l T r oy j oy j oi n t c oi n
f oi l oi l p oi n t b oy j oi n

foil joy loin coil Roy hoist
soil joint Troy boy point void
boil toy spoil coin joint foist
quoit joy Roy joint ploy coy

do **does**

Pals Once More

Joy had a new pal. Her pal was Bud, a boy in the house next to her. They **do** lots of things with wood. Bud made a skate board out of the wheels of a skate he had found and a plank that was cut from an oak tree. And it **does** work! Joy made some puppets out of boards and rags and chunks of shirts and pants. The puppets have joints, and they **do** work too. They make planes out of wood and tin foil. They **do** not work.

One day a bunch of kids from the next street came to ask Bud to join them to go fishing. This left Joy alone. At this point, it did not bother her too much, but when Bud went away with those kids day after day, it began to spoil her fun.

The next day when Joy woke up she had a big brain storm. She said to herself, "Bud **does** like to make things with you. How **do** you think you can get him to play with you as he once did? Joy, you can **do** it. Just wait and see!"

WHAT **DO** YOU THINK JOY DID TO MAKE BUD PLAY WITH HER? READ THE REST OF THE STORY AFTER YOUR NEXT LESSON.

Lesson 31 – Review

ar ay ou er oy
or ai ow ir oi
qu ur

f ar	c ar d	h ar p	sh ar k	l ar d	h ar d
w or n	b or n	c or k	f or k	n or th	sh or t
f ar	f or	c ar d	c or d	p or k	p ar k
h ow	d ow n	p l ow	c l ow n	ow l	f ow l
ou ch	f ou n d	sh ou t	p ou n d	p ou ch	s c ou t
p ai l	r ai d	ch ai n	p ay	p l ay	s t ay
qu i ck	qu ee n	qu i z	qu ake	qu a ck	qu i t
m ai l	s ay	qu ai l	g r ay	s t ai n	r ai n
t er m	v er b	p er t	j er k	p er ch	f er n
f ir m	g ir l	b ir ch	s ir	sh ir t	s t ir
ch ur ch	b ur n	h ur t	f ur	c ur l	b ur p
t oy	T r oy	s oy	b oy	R oy	j oy
s p oi l	b oi l	p oi n t	j oi n	j oi n t	oi l
f ar	f or	h ur l	g ir l	f ir s t	qu ite
p ai n	b oi l	p l ay	v er b	c ar d	h er
f ow l	qu i ck	b oy	ch ur n	h ar d	sh ou t
ur n	c oy	qu i z	ou ch	s oi l	f ar m
out	hail	quote	perch	store	turn
gray	coil	crowd	tray	start	stir
hoist	round	owl	toy	pray	start
short	turn	skirt	quick	frown	stout

Pals Once More (continued)

Joy said to herself, "Bud will want to play with you if he sees you make something big like a—like a—maybe like—a boat. No, a boat is too hard to make. Maybe a bird house. No, a bird house is not much. Quick now, what will it be? I have got it! Make a tree house."

There is a big oak tree in our yard that has lots of branches and Dad has lots of 2 by 4s and slabs of wood and other junk. He has big flat planks to stand on. We can make a house in the oak tree.

The next day when Bud came back to brag about his catch of fish he saw Joy going up the tree on a ladder she had made out of 2 by 4s. Bud said, "Joy, what are you going to make?"

Joy said, "I'm going to make a tree house. See the lumber I got from Dad. There is a fine spot up there to make a tree house. We can hoist the lumber up with a rope."

"That is neat!" said Bud. "I think Pete and Sam will help us."

"I will help too," said Pam. "I can hammer nails real well. May I bring a big blue tarp to cover the top? This will be a fine bunk house to play in."

So Pam, Pete, Sam, Bud, and Joy did a bang-up job. It took them all summer to make the tree house. Now Joy has lots of kids to play with and a good spot to play.

Test for Part II

* *To the teacher:* This test contains all the sounds taught in Part II. If the same sounds are responded to incorrectly twice, there is a need to reteach that sound.

dish
much
rock
moon
sheet
road
this
wheat
jaw
haunt
thing
bank
new
blue
gate
fine
rude
cope
star
born
stay
jail
couch

duck
loaf
shop
which
catch
lawn
long
pool
laud
seat
them
junk
clue
made
hope
dune
few
wide
march
play
north
brain
sound

clown
quit
verb
first
church
boy
oil

quick
brown
girl
her
curl
coin
coy

PART III

Consonant Blends and Other Shortcuts

Lesson 32

Beginning Consonant Blends

(sn)	s n ip	sn ob	sn ap	sn ore	sn eeze
(sw)	s w e ll	sw ing	sw eet	sw im	sw am
(sp)	s p urt	sp ort	sp ite	sp in	sp un
(sl)	s l ay	sl eek	sl ash	sl im	sl ot
(sk)	s k ip	sk ill	sk im	sk it	sk in
(sc)	s c at	sc ab	sc ore	sc amp	sc ar
(sm)	s m ell	sm ash	sm ack	sm ug	sm art
(st)	s t op	st ay	st ar	st ick	st ink

spill	skill	slit	spit	scab	spark
stake	snake	star	slit	skip	slip
spark	skin	snag	slime	smoke	stag

(fl)	f l oat	fl ag	fl at	fl ash	fl ush
(bl)	b l ot	bl eed	bl ess	bl ack	bl ock
(cl)	c l ean	cl ass	cl og	cl ay	cl ear
(gl)	g l eam	gl um	gl ass	gl ad	gl oat
(pl)	p l an	pl ay	pl ug	pl um	pl us

flip	clay	gloat	plate	float	black
clone	glad	flash	plum	clock	clean
fled	bleed	plug	gleam	flag	Glen

slush	sport	glass	flush	swam	star
flack	blade	clap	click	plush	class
smart	skip	sneeze	slap	bless	plan

Lesson 33

More Beginning Consonant Blends

(br)	b r at	br ing	br ag	br ain	br ick
(cr)	c r ab	cr eek	cr ash	cr ush	cr ib
(dr)	d r ip	dr op	dr ug	dr um	dr ess
(fr)	f r esh	fr et	Fr ed	fr ock	fr ee
(pr)	p r ess	pr op	pr om	pr ick	pr ay
(tr)	t r ain	tr uck	tr ail	tr eat	tr ip

pray	grin	from	drum	grip	broke
drape	brave	crate	drab	brim	dress
brake	tray	grade	grime	trade	prom

clash	crash	flock	frock	bleed	breed
glass	grass	play	pray	clash	crash
flesh	fresh	flee	free	plop	prop

smash	track	score	smoke	block	play
train	slot	smell	clean	plan	bleed
creek	brain	skill	scar	smack	snore
press	scab	fresh	smoke	spark	brag

Lesson 34

Common Syllables with -nd

(and)	and	s and	b and	h and	l and
	gr and	br and	st and	bl and	gl and
(end)	end	s end	b end	bl end	sp end
	l end	m end	t end	f end	tr end
(ond)	f ond	p ond	b ond	fr ond	bl ond
	p ond	b ond	bl ond	f ond	fr ond
(ind)	f ind	bl ind	gr ind	k ind	m ind
	b ind	h ind	w ind	r ind	f ind
(ound)	f ound	s ound	r ound	b ound	h ound
	m ound	w ound	p ound	gr ound	f ound

and	end	m end	m ound	p ond	p ound
b ound	b and	b end	bl end	bl and	br and
s and	s end	s ound	f ound	f ond	f ind
gr and	gr ind	gr ound	l end	l and	bl and

blend	gland	pound	fend	land	blind
find	lend	grand	round	mend	brand
sand	grind	found	stand	fond	tend
kind	sound	spend	hand	mound	hound

Lesson 35

Common Syllables with -nt

(ant)	ant	r ant	sl ant	ch ant	pl ant
	p ant	c ant	gr ant	sc ant	sl ant
(ent)	t ent	s ent	r ent	sp ent	w ent
	b ent	l ent	d ent	p ent	Br ent
(int)	m int	t int	h int	l int	pr int
	gl int	fl int	st int	sp l int	sp r int
(unt)	h unt	r unt	st unt	gr unt	bl unt
	b unt	p unt	r unt	br unt	sh unt

r ent	r ant	l ent	l int	p ent	p ant
h int	h unt	s ent	sp ent	ant	d ent
t ent	t int	gr ant	gr unt	b ent	b unt

runt	tint	lent	rant	sent	hint
dent	stunt	rent	slant	lint	grunt
pent	chant	spent	plant	went	brunt
tent	bent	mint	hunt	print	sprint
spent	print	dint	pant	splint	shunt

Lesson 36

Common Syllables with -nch and -mp

(anch)	r anch	br anch	bl anch	st anch	g anch
(ench)	b ench	fr ench	dr ench	tr ench	cl ench
(inch)	inch	p inch	fl inch	gr inch	cl inch
(unch)	l unch	br unch	b unch	m unch	cr unch

b unch	b ench	fr ench	fl inch	cl inch	gr inch
p inch	p unch	r anch	m unch	br anch	dr ench
brunch	branch	stanch	stench	lunch	trench
clench	crunch	drench	punch	flinch	ranch

(amp)	c amp	l amp	d amp	st amp	ch amp
	tr amp	cl amp	r amp	cr amp	st amp
(imp)	l imp	bl imp	ch imp	cr imp	pr imp
(ump)	l ump	b ump	d ump	j ump	st ump

ch amp	ch imp	ch ump	l amp	l imp	l ump
d amp	d ump	st amp	st ump	cr amp	cr imp
plump	thump	tramp	trump	rump	ramp

bump	chimp	lamp	ranch	blimp	drench
trench	ramp	crunch	stamp	flinch	champ
clench	branch	slump	inch	primp	clinch
brunch	tramp	thump	champ	lunch	bench

Lesson 37 — Review

Beginning Consonant Blends and Common Syllables

bl and	gr and	st and	sp end	tr end	bl end
f ond	fr ond	bl ond	f ound	gr ound	h ound
pl ant	sl ant	gr ant	sp ent	s ent	Tr ent
pr int	st int	fl int	st unt	bl unt	gr unt
br anch	st anch	bl anch	fr ench	cl ench	tr ench
cl inch	fl inch	w inch	br unch	cr unch	bunch
cl amp	cr amp	cr imp	bl imp	pl ump	tr ump

hand	chant	went	clamp	skate	ground
stick	flint	band	stunt	skimp	found
kind	brand	trend	pinch	blind	still
smash	scar	crunch	grind	lunch	bound
bland	ranch	gleam	sweet	smash	mind
bump	bench	punch	blimp	brand	primp
went	round	ranch	lamp	sprint	spark

Lesson 38

Word Ending Blends

(-lk)	ilk	m ilk	s ilk	b ilk
	s ulk	b ulk	h ulk	sk ulk
(-lt)	t ilt	st ilt	l ilt	qu ilt
	b elt	m elt	f elt	p elt
(-ld)	h eld	w eld	m eld	g eld
(-lp)	h elp	k elp	y elp	wh elp
(-lf)	elf	s elf	sh elf	d elf

m ilk	m elt	m eld	h ulk	h eld	h elp
b elt	b ulk	s ulk	s elf	sh elf	st ilt
f elt	v ault	qu ilt	s ilk	f ault	h ilt

felt	self	meld	shelf	fault	help
quilt	hulk	vault	sulk	self	kelp
held	belt	milk	weld	silk	stilt
delf	smelt	skulk	yelp	melt	fault
whelp	scalp	bilk	stilt	kelp	Alp

Lesson 39

More Word Ending Blends

(-ct)	act	f act	p act	t act
	s ect	d uct	st r ict	tr act
(-ft)	r aft	sh aft	dr aft	cr aft
	l ift	g ift	dr ift	sh ift
(-pt)	sl ept	k ept	w ept	cr ept
	apt	r apt	opt	a d opt
(-st)	b est	w est	ch est	cr est
	l ist	tw ist	f ist	m ist

act	apt	l ift	l eft	dr ift	dr aft
p act	p est	cr aft	cr est	cr ept	ch est
r aft	r apt	sh ift	sh aft	gr aft	gr ist
t ack	t act	z est	s ect	sl ept	st r ict

kept	cleft	pact	twist	crept	quest
draft	fact	strict	adopt	slept	mist
grist	nest	rapt	left	act	tract
tractor	stricter	drifter	actor	copter	twister

Lesson 40

Blends of 3 Letters

(thr)	th r ee	thr ee	th r ive	thr ive
	th r ong	thr oat	thr ive	thr ust
	th r one	thr ob	thr ill	thr ee
(shr)	sh r unk	shr unk	sh r ine	shr ine
	sh r ub	shr ug	shr ed	shr imp
	sh r ink	shr ank	shr ill	shr ewd
(squ)	s qu aw	squ aw	s qu ire	squ ire
	s qu int	squ irt	squ eak	squ eal
	s qu id	squ int	squ irm	squ awk

shr ank   thr ob   squ eeze   thr oat   squ eak
thr ill   shr ug   squ irt   thr ive   thr ust
thr ee   shr ink   shr imp   squ eal   thr ong

throne   shrub   squint   shrink   throb
throat   shrank   three   squeeze   shrine
shrug   shred   thrust   shrimp   squeak
squaw   thrive   squid   throb   squirt

Lesson 41

More Blends of 3 Letters

(scr)	s c r unch	scr unch	s c r ibe	scr ibe
	s c r een	scr eam	scr ap	scr am
	s c r atch	scr ub	scr ew	scr ape
(spr)	s p r ee	spr ee	s p r ang	spr ang
	s p r ain	spr ay	spr ing	spr out
	s p r ite	spr int	spr ig	spr awl
(spl)	s p l ay	spl ay	s p l int	spl int
	s p l ash	spl it	spl een	spl otch
	s p l its	spl at	spl ice	spl ints
(str)	s t r ay	str ay	s t r ain	str ain
	s t r eak	str eet	str ipe	str ing
	s t r ap	str and	str eam	str eet

spr ing	str ing	scr eam	str eam	str ap	scr ap
spl otch	scr atch	scr ew	str aw	scr ibe	str ide
spl int	spr int	str ay	spr ay	scr een	spl een

splash	straw	street	sprout	scram	strain
spring	stray	splint	stream	scrub	scratch
sprain	split	splotch	strut	stroke	screen
stripe	spray	strap	splash	splinter	streamer

Lesson 42 — Review

Word Ending Blends and Blends of 3 Letters

m ilk	s ilk	s ulk	st ilt	qu ilt	b elt
h eld	w eld	g eld	sh elf	s elf	elf
h elp	k elp	y elp	wh elp	y elp	h elp
act	d uct	tr act	sh aft	dr ift	r aft
sl ept	k ept	w ept	r apt	apt	opt
f ist	tw ist	gr ist	bl est	ch est	cr est
thr ee	thr oat	thr ust	thr ob	thr ill	thr ong
shr ug	shr ink	shr imp	shr ine	shr ub	shr ank
squ eal	squ id	squ eak	squ int	squ aw	squ eeze
scr een	scr eam	scr ub	spr ee	spr ing	spr ay
spl it	spl een	spl otch	str ain	str ipe	str ong
grist	screen	squawk	sulk	welder	silk
held	duct	twister	shaft	drift	adrift
spray	yelp	three	shrimp	thrust	squint
split	dweller	shrug	scrape	blest	smell
unheld	induct	twist	quest	splinter	skulking

Test for Part III

* *To the teacher:* This test contains all the sounds taught in Part III. If the same sounds are responded to incorrectly twice, there is a need to reteach that sound.

sport	brain
smash	class
clean	smell
bring	spurt
found	punt
mind	pound
hunt	find
lunch	lamp
camp	bunch
melt	wept
kept	belt
spring	shred
shrine	glad
glass	spray
press	went
rent	prop
lump	shelf
self	bump
raft	split
three	gift
splash	throb

PART IV

New Configurations

Lesson 43

Short Words Ending in -y or -ie

by my why thy shy sky
fry try pry cry dry sty
fly ply sly spy spry shy
rely supply reply defy standby deny

lie pie tie die fie hie
died tied tried spied fried relied
tie tied die died try tried
spy spied ply plied dry dried
lie lied deny denied supply supplied

deny spy lie why sly spy
fried mudpie die spry lied ply
tried defy by standby spied belie
pie untie pigsty supplied reply sky

Lesson 44

oll old olt

r oll	t oll	tr oll	str oll	scr oll
boll	droll	poll	rolling	unroll
old	c old	h old	t old	m old
bold	sold	scold	fold	gold
c olt	b olt	j olt	m olt	v olt
dolt	molten	unbolt	jolting	revolt
toll	told	boll	bold	bolt
cold	colt	droll	dolt	old
mold	molt	unfold	unroll	unbolt
volt	sold	troll	hold	molten
unfold	droll	bolt	rolling	sold
jolt	old	told	scroll	bolder
scold	gold	tollroad	golden	older
roller	stroller	folder	jolting	unrolling

Lesson 45

kn gn wr

kn ee	kn ife	kn it	kn ew	kn ot	
knife	knave	knell	knock	knead	
knoll	knots	kneel	knack	knob	
gn aw	gn ash	gn at	gn ome		
gnarl	gnat	gnaw	gnawing		
wr ite	wr ong	wr ing	wr en	wr it	
wrench	wrote	wrung	written	wrap	
wrinkle	wreck	wreath	wrangle	wrist	
knit	writ	gnaw	knew	knot	gnat
write	knife	wrong	gnome	knack	wreck
ring	wring	not	knot	wrung	rung
knot	gnarl	knob	wrench	write	
gnash	knock	gnaw	wreck	wriggle	
gnat	knife	wrote	knit	gnome	
wrong	knob	gnats	wring	knell	
gnash	writ	wrinkle	knocks	wrist	
written	knew	gnaws	wrap	gnawing	

Lesson 46

all alt

all	b all	f all	t all	c all	w all
stall	small	hall	squall	pall	mall

s alt	h alt	m alt	W alt
exalt	basalt	Walter	smalt

hall	halt	mall	malt	salt	squall
small	smalt	wall	Walt	stale	stall
mall	small	tall	stall	hall	halt

all	stall	salt	halting	fallen	exalt
tall	smaller	salted	ball	malt	call
fallen	taller	wall	halt	wall	small
hall	Walter	squall	hallway	falter	downfall

Lesson 47

alk -mb ph

w alk	t alk	b alk	ch alk	st alk
walker	talking	balks	catwalk	stalking
l amb	l imb	c omb	cl imb	b omb
d umb	th umb	cr umb	n umb	th umb
ph one	ph lox	Ph il	ph oo ey	ph an ta sy
ne phew	ph an tom	ph on ics	Ral ph	gra ph
balk	climb	phone	lamb	graph
phlox	crumb	stalks	Phil	nephew
limb	Ralph	bomb	phantom	talking
phooey	dumb	comb	thumb	phlox
walk	phone	limb	talking	Ralph
stalk	numb	phantasy	crumb	phonics
bomb	elephant	phlox	climber	combing
Phil	telephone	nephew	balk	physics
telegraph	Philip	thumb	catwalk	phantom

Lesson 48 — Review

-y old kn all alk
-ie oll gn alt -mb
olt wr ph

why	spry	shy	rely	fry
tie	lie	died	pie	denied
old	hold	scold	sold	told
roll	troll	stroll	roll	scroll
colt	volt	bolt	revolt	jolt
knock	knot	knit	knew	knee
gnaw	gnash	gnat	gnome	gnarl
write	wrench	wrong	wrote	wriggle
call	stall	mall	tall	small
Walt	malt	salt	falter	halting
walk	stalk	chalk	balk	talking
climb	dumb	crumb	numb	comb
phone	Phil	graph	phantom	telephone
wrote	chalk	cried	asphalt	gnash
lamb	walk	phone	wrench	scold
wriggle	knock	fold	ball	stalk
wrong	squall	halter	knee	Walter
limb	plied	dry	troll	revolt
died	knead	gnaw	supplied	standby

Lesson 49

Final -y and -ly

funn y	bunn y	sunn y	runn y	penn y	
happy	snappy	scrappy	puppy	guppy	
needy	greedy	seedy	weedy	speedy	
sassy	classy	glassy	grassy	fussy	
twenty	thirty	forty	fifty	sixty	
chil ly	hil ly	sil ly	Bil ly	Sal ly	
simply	pimply	dimply	limply	amply	
dolly	holly	Molly	golly	folly	
dust	dusty	hand	handy	dusk	dusky
dirt	dirty	rain	rainy	salt	salty
bad	badly	cold	coldly	hard	hardly
short	shortly	new	newly	frank	frankly
kindly	quickly	gladly	rainy	nasty	mainly
dandy	rally	pantry	nicely	thirty	slowly
forty	funny	scrappy	greedy	Billy	sixty
lucky	weekly	lonely	strongly	inky	blankly
mainly	shortly	porky	grouchy	perky	pointy

Lesson 50

ce ci cy

ace	p ace	f ace	pl ace	r ace
space	brace	lace	grace	trace
ice	mice	rice	nice	dice
price	twice	dice	spice	lice
sin ce	min ce	prin ce	win ce	quin ce
France	chance	glance	prance	dance
fence	pence	hence	thence	whence
cent	cede	center	city	cite
cell	circle	cigar	cinch	celery
cinder	circus	citizen	Cinderella	central
Nan cy	fan cy	chan cy	floun cy	bouncy
since	lace	cinch	France	cinder
prance	spice	pence	circus	bouncy
mice	slice	quince	celery	cigar
trace	chance	fancy	glance	nice
cents	central	whence	twice	cite

Lesson 51

gi ge se

age	p age	r age	st age	w age
edge	wedge	ledge	forge	gorge
fudge	judge	smudge	grudge	budge
urge	surge	purge	splurge	merge
dodge	lodge	ridge	bridge	Midge

gin	ginger	giraffe	gem	germ
George	Georgia	gentle	gel	gentlemen

n ose	r ose	cl ose	ch ose	p ose
ease	easy	please	tease	cheese

forge	badge	fringe	wages	close
budge	use	ginger	smudge	pledge
Georgia	page	backstage	chose	gorge
large	surge	stage	purge	bridge
please	gently	ginger	noise	backstage

Lesson 52

ook ood

b ook	l ook	sh ook	h ook	c ook
nook	rook	took	brook	crook
outlook	forsook	looking	bookcase	bookmark

g ood	h ood	st ood	w ood	g ood
Robin Hood	manhood	withstood	Hollywood	goodness

hook	hood	shook	stood	crook
booklet	forsook	hooks	woods	bookend
rook	woodbox	outlook	withstood	woodchuck
lookout	nook	wooden	Brookline	Robin Hood
goodness	Hollywood	goodby	manhood	took

Lesson 53 — Review

-y ce ge ook
-ly ci gi ood
cy se

funny	thirty	speedy	happy	puppy
dolly	badly	newly	frankly	dimply
place	rice	spice	trace	twice
since	dance	pence	glance	chance
cigar	circle	celery	cell	cent
judge	wedge	George	stage	gentlemen
ginger	gin	giraffe	gigantic	ginseng
please	noise	fuse	pose	cheese
took	brook	bookmark	cook	forsook
goodness	wood	hoods	withstood	Hollywood

bookend	central	merger	poise	mainly
twenty	easy	splice	giraffe	use
Georgia	splurge	dolly	happy	whence
glance	scrappy	tease	germs	closed
hooks	bouncy	France	barge	strongly
grassy	Billy	goodby	forge	shortly

Lesson 54

The lazy final -e

h ou se	m ou se	l ou se	sp ou se	bl ou se
loose	goose	moose	noose	caboose
solve	starve	twelve	delve	shelve
nurse	purse	curse	verse	horse
apple	dapple	amble	gamble	ample
tickle	sickle	chuckle	buckle	uncle
tense	dense	sense	expense	defense
tumble	fumble	mumble	pebble	bubble
wiggle	waggle	haggle	struggle	juggle

douse	curve	bottle	sickle	caboose
chuckle	Morse	grumble	candle	apple
mouse	moose	pebble	settle	defense
expanse	solves	swerve	mouse	verse
simple	babble	terse	scramble	juggle
dribble	humble	starve	grapple	course

Lesson 55

-igh -ight

s igh	h igh	n igh	th igh	h igh
sight	might	night	light	tight
knight	fight	right	fright	bright
flight	plight	blight	slight	might
sigh	sight	slight	slightly	slighter
light	lights	lighter	lightly	lightening
night	knight	might	right	tight
fight	fights	fighter	fright	frighten
sighing	brighter	slightest	lighten	slightly
night	brighten	flight	highly	knights
fighting	mighty	blight	frighten	thigh
highway	highroad	highlight	highness	hightail
highland	highchair	highboy	higher	highjump
daylight	sunlight	moonlight	lamplight	starlight
flashlight	highlight	lighten	lightening	nightlight

Lesson 56

ie

ch ie f	gr ie f	br ie f	be l ie f	re l ie f
field	wield	shield	yield	wielder
niece	piece	priest	priestess	pieces
tier	pier	pierce	fierce	piers

thief	relief	disbelief	siege	besiege
fierce	Brownie	fiend	thief	lien
Winnie	Annie	Carrie	Maggie	eerie
carried	married	tarried	relief	relieve
shielding	achieve	grieve	infield	outfield
nieces	debrief	handkerchief	relieve	buried

Lesson 57

eigh aught
eight ought

w eigh	sl eigh	n eigh	a w eigh	w eigh s
eight	eighteen	eighty	eighty	eighteenth
freight	freighter	freightage	freighting	freighters
neigh	neighbor	neighbors	neighborhood	neighboring
sleigh	eighteen	freighter	weigh	eighty
neigh	eight	neighborhood	weigh	eighteenth
aught	c aught	t aught	fr aught	n aught
daughter	slaughter	naughty	distraught	manslaughter
ought	n ought	s ought	th ought	b ought
brought	fought	rought	thoughtful	thoughtless

ought	aught	thought	taught	fought	fraught
nought	naught	brought	naughty	daughter	wrought

weight	bought	freight	naughty	sleigh
wrought	thoughtful	eighteen	daughter	caught
neighborhood	sought	brought	distraught	freightage

Lesson 58 — Review

Final -e -igh ie eigh aught
-ight eight ought

solve	amble	chuckle	moose	wiggle
high	sigh	thigh	highjump	nigh
knight	right	tighter	moonlight	flight
niece	fierce	relief	lien	wielder
eighteen	weigh	freighter	sleigh	eighty
daughter	naughty	taught	distraught	caught
ought	brought	thoughtful	fought	nought

dense	sight	grief	weigh	sickle
blight	thief	naught	freighter	delve
caboose	highchair	disbelief	neighbor	outfield
buried	verse	goose	blight	achieve
Maggie	ought	spouse	daylight	carried
moose	married	wields	piers	lighter

Test for Part IV

* *To the teacher:* This test contains all the sounds taught in Part IV. If the same sounds are responded to incorrectly twice, there is a need to reteach that sound.

fry	small	weigh	fought
die	talk	eighty	taught
scroll	graph	caught	freight
cold	grassy	brought	sleigh
bolt	nice	nose	uncle
tall	dry		
salt	comb		
walk	roll		
dumb	simply		
phone	lie		
penny	dolt		
shortly	cell		
face	told		
cent	exalt		
fancy	ledge		
stage	booklet		
gem	wooden		
goodness	bouncy		
crook	germ		
buckle	bright		
high	yield		
right	sigh		
brief	rose		

PART V

Exceptions to Configurations Previously Taught

Lesson 59

ea th (unvoiced)

h ea d	d ea d	r ea d	l ea d	dr ea d
tread	bread	thread	stead	spread
deaf	sweat	sweater	realm	meant
weather	leather	feather	heather	feathers
heavy	heaven	leaven	heavily	readiness
steady	ready	readily	deadly	sweating
ahead	behead	instead	steady	steadily
ba th	pa th	ha th	ma th	wra th
Smith	fifth	sixth	eighth	ninth
mirth	birth	filth	forth	wealth
north	south	mouth	tooth	seventh
th ink	th ank	th ick	th ird	th ing
throat	throne	three	thorn	thirty
threw	throw	throng	thrash	theme
sweater	heaven	throne	bath	third
south	instead	meant	tooth	thing
thumb	spread	leather	sixth	ready
sweater	think	mirth	north	bread
thimble	heavy	realm	deadly	three

Lesson 60

Words Ending in -o, -oe, and -ow

hello	ago	zero	also	poncho
patio	piano	potato	domino	gusto
radio	tomato	buffalo	Eskimo	torpedo

toe	woe	foe	doe	Joe
floe	hoe	throe	oboe	roe

low	sow	tow	mow	show
slow	flow	glow	blow	grow
crow	grow	snow	below	follow
shadow	elbow	rainbow	blown	grown

hello	pillow	shown	grower	oboe
Joe	tomato	pillow	slower	patio
snowball	snowman	snowflake	snowstorm	snowing
domino	buffalo	minnow	blowing	poncho
rowboat	follow	zero	also	hollow
memento	torpedo	widow	Tokyo	foes

Lesson 61

-ive -ous

give	forgive	active	captive	attentive
passive	massive	pensive	festive	respective
expensive	expansive	live	outlive	liver
joy ous	murder ous	nerv ous	gener ous	por ous
marvelous	tremendous	mountainous	raucous	bulbous
amorous	ponderous	luminous	venemous	disastrous
captive	nervous	bulbous	forgive	attentive
generous	tremendous	respective	massive	cavernous
luminous	festive	plaintive	decorous	amorous
extensive	onerous	joyous	active	mountainous
bulbous	pensive	outlive	sonorous	disastrous

Lesson 62

-ull other

b ull	p ull	f ull	f ull y	f ull ness
bullfight	bullet	bullfrog	bulldog	bulldoze
pullet	pulley	pulling	pullup	pulled
other	m other	br other	sm other	an other
otherwise	brotherly	mothers	smothering	someother
noneother	motherland	others	motherly	brother-in-law
bulletin	otherwise	fullback	pulley	mother-in-law
another	playful	smother	bullet	anyother
fullness	pullup	brothers	motherly	fully
bulldog	fullback	someother	bulldoze	otherworld
motherland	brotherhood	fuller	fullgrown	pullet

Lesson 63

over even

over	cl over	R over	D over	St over
overjoy	overcoat	overtake	overlook	overturn
overtime	overlap	overwork	overnight	moreover
overseas	overalls	overthrow	overhaul	overhead

even	St even	un even	even ing	even tide
evensong	evenhanded	evenly	evener	evenness

moreover	evening	Steven	overcoat	Dover
overnight	evenly	overturn	overlap	eventide
clover	overjoy	overnight	uneven	overseas
evenly	overthrow	overhead	evensong	overlook

Lesson 64 — Review

ea -o -ive -ull over
th -oe -ous other even
-ow

dead	read	spread	meant	leather
bath	sixth	tooth	third	throat
patio	tomato	also	poncho	radio
toe	hoe	oboe	doe	throe
crow	elbow	below	grown	follow
active	liver	outlive	passive	forgive
joyous	raucous	porous	luminous	murderous
bullet	fully	pulley	mother	another
overjoy	moreover	overhaul	evening	evener
bulldog	overturn	marvelous	throne	bread
foes	blown	motherland	hollow	snowflake
memento	overalls	expensive	fuller	generous
snowstorm	domino	rainbow	brothers	respective
eventide	bullish	zero	nervous	leather
ninth	north	minnow	fullback	clover

Test for Part V

* *To the teacher:* This test contains all the sounds taught in Part V. If the same sounds are responded to incorrectly twice, there is a need to reteach that sound.

sweat	evenly
fifth	below
also	meant
doe	north
follow	active
forgive	hoe
joyous	bullet
fully	generous
mother	overhead
overturn	others
evening	zero

PART VI

Word Building and Syllabication

Lesson 65

Plural -s and -es

cat	cats	girl	girls	cup	cups
boy	boys	other	others	shop	shops
feel	feels	see	sees	make	makes
smell	smells	hurt	hurts	hate	hates

dress	dresses	glass	glasses	brush	brushes
ditch	ditches	witch	witches	patch	patches
bless	blesses	press	presses	pass	passes
wish	wishes	smash	smashes	rush	rushes

phones	crumbs	wrenches	holds	gnashes	switches
fusses	stretches	chances	pages	pleases	twitches
matches	circles	houses	brothers	gashes	reaches
weighs	solves	ranches	feathers	baths	batches
mothers	flushes	paths	patches	nights	bulldogs
hatches	glasses	dresses	follows	evenings	weeks

Lesson 66

Possessive 's and Contractions

Mike	Mike's	Dick	Dick's	Pat	Pat's
Bob	Bob's	Meg	Meg's	Dick	Dick's
man	man's	king	king's	chimp	chimp's
bird	bird's	mother	mother's	cowboy	cowboy's
she is	she's	he is	he's	that is	that's
can not	can't	did not	didn't	is not	isn't
was not	wasn't	could not	couldn't	were not	weren't
we will	we'll	she will	she'll	I will	I'll
he would	he'd	we would	we'd	they would	they'd
Steven's	they'll	there's	mouse's	Joe's	they'd
Maggie's	Jenny's	wasn't	we'll	aren't	Eskimo's
wouldn't	queen's	farmer's	I'd	giant's	weren't
she's	Chad's	skunk's	swan's	isn't	he's
that's	camper's	we'd	isn't	runner's	tractor's

Lesson 67

Past tense -ed

rain	rain ed	play	play ed	chew	chew ed
dreamed	smelled	jumped	needed	helped	rushed
taste	tast ed	skate	skat ed	glue	glu ed
liked	wasted	shared	hoped	smiled	choked
stop	stopp ed	jog	jogg ed	drop	dropp ed
robbed	clipped	grabbed	mugged	batted	shopped
choked	slapped	sneezed	skipped	floated	grinned
prayed	handed	planted	lunched	scraped	rolled
talked	phoned	raced	circled	posed	cooked
teased	starved	solved	juggled	weighed	headed
hoed	pulled	followed	painted	roped	dined

Lesson 68

Suffix -ing

fish	fish ing	fly	fly ing	park	park ing
going	saying	selling	waiting	meaning	feeling
sit	sitt ing	run	runn ing	hum	humm ing
planning	spinning	starring	cutting	grinning	digging
smoke	smok ing	ride	rid ing	make	mak ing
smiling	hoping	shaking	firing	wiping	biting
winning	biting	marching	drawing	playing	nailing
rolling	shouting	plowing	stirring	sailing	boiling
walking	moping	hosing	climbing	merging	closing
selling	tickling	juggling	scolding	lighting	sighing
hopping	smiling	raining	heading	thinking	giving

Lesson 69

Comparatives
er est

old	old er	old est	slow	slow er	slow est
long	longer	longest	high	higher	highest
big	bigg er	bigg est	hot	hott er	hott est
sad	sadder	saddest	wet	wetter	wettest
cute	cut er	cut est	fine	fin er	fin est
late	lat er	lat est	true	tru er	tru est
fresher	freer	highest	sanest	sweeter	slowest
tamest	flatter	smartest	braver	greenest	blinder
darkest	lighter	rounder	hardest	coolest	cheaper
thinnest	stronger	newer	madder	rudest	bluest
poorest	higher	lamer	flattest	slowest	ruder

Lesson 70 — Review

Plural -s & -es, Possessive 's, Contractions, Past tense -ed, Suffix -ing, & Comparatives

smells	hates	sees	brushes	fusses	rushes
Dick's	Pat's	man's	girl's	wasn't	there's
jumped	needed	liked	hoped	robbed	dropped
fishing	doing	sitting	digging	shaking	tiring
longer	highest	biggest	wetter	later	finest

glasses	weren't	shared	poorest	juggling	liked
we'll	twitches	sadder	sailing	sneezed	Sam's
couldn't	witches	wasted	thinner	posed	jumped
they'd	grabbed	boiling	makes	bullfrogs	evened
cowboy's	smuggled	darker	stirring	cheapest	aren't
mothers	poked	tamest	selling	we'll	gluing

Lesson 71

re- be- de- pre-

re pay	re read	re move	re run	re place
return	remark	remind	report	recall
remain	relax	reduce	refine	reform
be hind	be long	be side	be fall	be tween
beyond	behave	begin	began	begun
below	believe	before	beware	betray
de part	de pend	de feat	de face	de vote
device	detest	deform	demand	denote
defend	define	degree	debate	delight
pre tend	pre cise	pre fer	pre dict	pre vent
prepaid	prepare	prefix	pretend	preshrunk
pretense	prevail	prescribe	prelude	preheat
reform	devour	prefer	between	return
remind	depend	prevent	deform	predict
belong	below	retire	detest	repeat
befall	belief	delight	prevent	relax
degrade	between	precise	prescribe	behold

Lesson 72

com con pro dis

com bat	com et	com ic	com ma	com mon
compact	complex	compound	comrade	comment
con ceal	con cern	con fess	con sult	con tain
confirm	content	consent	confide	conform
dis cuss	dis gust	dis grace	dis card	dis cord
discreet	disturb	disperse	display	dismiss
pro tect	pro vide	pro test	pro noun	pro gram
propose	produce	promote	profile	proclaim
comrade	profound	prohibit	dislike	content
confide	propel	dismay	consent	display
discern	container	concerning	propeller	comrade
confess	disturb	compound	consult	proposal
confide	compact	program	discreet	discount

Lesson 73

-sion -tion -ation -ution

pen sion	pas sion	ses sion	mis sion	ex pan sion
admission	confession	permission	discussion	expression
profession	emission	fission	aggression	compassion
ac tion	dic tion	fic tion	ad di tion	con di tion
intention	fraction	petition	ambition	position
ammunition	nutrition	tradition	detention	ignition
n ation	st ation	cre ation	sens ation	form ation
ration	relation	donation	admiration	inflation
foundation	information	plantation	deflation	starvation
sol ution	dil ution	poll ution	exec ution	revol ution
evolution	distribution	contribution	constitution	
institution	persecution	prosecution	pollution	
munition	flirtation	passion	execution	institution
inflation	nutrition	session	relation	creation
expansion	omission	solution	pension	tradition
nation	plantation	foundation	edition	detention
fission	admiration	execution	dilution	fraction

Lesson 74

Compound Words

for ever	whenever	however	whatever	everyone
up set	upstairs	uphill	upon	upward
down town	downhill	downfall	downstairs	downward
over look	overturn	overjoy	overwork	overgrown
with hold	within	withstand	withdraw	without
rain coat	rainstorm	rainbow	raindrop	rainfall
sun set	sunrise	sunshine	sundown	sunburn
side show	sideline	sidewalk	sideway	sidetrack
every day	everything	everywhere	everybody	everyone
any place	anytime	anywhere	anyone	anyhow

sometime	upward	herself	rainbow	without
sunshine	sideline	overturn	downturn	upstairs
Sunday	backfire	daytime	sunlight	everyone
seaside	bookcase	rainfall	whatever	without
ourselves	upward	forever	background	airport

Lesson 75

Two Syllable Words

la dy	ti ny	tu lip	cra zy	gra vy
pilot	poison	cradle	broken	triple
native	plaza	bonus	cable	super
mag net	pub lic	ab sent	en ter	con voy
cactus	velvet	garden	forest	apron
after	monkey	silver	simple	tender
ham mer	slip per	pup pet	dif fer	bot tle
ribbon	narrow	pepper	tennis	rabbit
pillow	rubber	puzzle	button	errand
struggle	student	motor	staple	bonus
blister	monkey	yellow	cactus	forest
tiny	sparkle	stable	broken	follow
stupid	narrow	rubber	velvet	simple
rapid	muzzle	bottle	magnet	farther

Lesson 76

Three & Four Syllable Words

ra di o	en e my	com e dy	ster e o	cel er y
pioneer	cabinet	accident	democrat	electric
carnival	porcupine	romantic	submarine	hospital
parachute	minister	medicine	marvelous	happiness

i den ti fy	de liv er y	op er a tion	ter ri to ry
solitary	imitation	independent	refrigerate
investigate	ammunition	discovery	manufacture
presentation	preposition	reservation	constitution

submarine	pioneer	ammunition	discovery
carnival	cabinet	establishment	slippery
romantic	accident	proposition	comparison
marvelous	parachute	republican	solitary
manufacture	hospital	parachute	recovery

Lesson 75—Review

Compound Words—Multisyllabic Words

re-	com-	-sion
be-	con-	-tion
de-	pro-	-ation
precede	dis-	-ution

refine
common
addition
rainstorm
tennis
solitary

beyond
contend
inflation
without
bottle
radio

defend
provide
passion
sunlight
magnet
identity

prepaid
discuss
solution
daytime
rabbit
romantic

delight
consult
ignition
backfire
pilot
hospital

action
carnival
consent
parachute
broken

discern
between
creation
discount
delivery

overjoy
proclaim
sometime
pollution
preshrunk

repeat
marvelous
prescribe
everyone
compound

farther
investigation
cactus
foundation
plantation

Test for Part VI

* *To the teacher:* This test contains all the sounds taught in Part VI. If the same sounds are responded to incorrectly twice, there is a need to reteach that sound.

glasses	grabbed
I'd	latest
liked	device
planning	witches
hottest	discard
prefix	profession
program	wasn't
sensation	background
ourselves	smoking
native	territory
reservation	gravy
Bob's	preheat
deface	beyond
begin	horses
repeat	remark
display	confide
conceal	combat
mission	execution